RIDING
A BEGINNER'S GUIDE

RIDING
A BEGINNER'S GUIDE

Stef Eardley BHSII, MScES and Stephanie Bateman BSc Hons

J. A. ALLEN · LONDON

First published in 2014 by
J. A. Allen
Clerkenwell House
Clerkenwell Green
London EC1R 0HT

J. A. Allen is an imprint of Robert Hale Limited
www.allenbooks.co.uk

ISBN 978-1-908809-23-0

British Library in Cataloging Data
A catalogue record for this book is available from the British Library

Edited by Martin Diggle
Designed and typeset by Paul Saunders
Photographs by Mike Bateman
Line drawings by Carole Vincer
Printed by Craft Print International Ltd, Singapore

Disclaimer of Liability
The authors and publisher shall have neither liability nor responsibility to
any person or entity with respect to any loss or damage caused or alleged to
be caused directly or indirectly by the information contained in this book.
While the book is as accurate as the authors can make it, there may be errors,
omissions, and inaccuracies.

CONTENTS

ACKNOWLEDGEMENTS

With thanks to:

Kirsty Chaplin and April Style

Hannah Fenech and April Dantzer

Jenni Fenech and April Masterpiece

Sebastian Curran and Van Damme

Izabela Motyl and Freddie

Jess Williams and Rocco

Fran Peszynska and Archie

Darcy Murphy and Joker

Sam Bradshaw and Orro

Steph Bateman and Tess

Kate Justice and Simba

William Justice and Dolly

Libby Justice and Rooster

Hartpury College

Ashleworth Centre of Equestrian Services

Thalia Edwards BSc ESS, ORC Dip SMP, ITEC Dip ESMP

Molly Tombs

INTRODUCTION

'No hour of life is wasted that is spent in the saddle.'
WINSTON CHURCHILL

With over 3.5 million riders in the UK according to the most recent British Equestrian Trade Association national survey, there must be something about horse riding that attracts people to this activity. Perhaps it's being outdoors in the fresh air, enjoying the countryside and spending time with a beautiful, intelligent animal. Or maybe it is the feeling of freedom when you're sat astride such a powerful and fast-moving animal. It's hard not to see the horse's appeal, even to non-riders.

So what exactly is it about riding that people love? Ask any rider why they enjoy riding and they will answer with a multitude of reasons: it relieves stress; it makes them happy; they enjoy the partnership with their horse; it gives them a sense of responsibility; it keeps them active and healthy. Nearly all riders will share the common belief that once they meet a horse, they become addicted for life.

Whether you want to compete for your country or simply enjoy the delights of the countryside from horseback, riding is not only good for your health, but for you mind and soul too.

You are never too young or old to learn to ride. At whatever stage you are in your life, riding is never out of reach for anyone. Some people

Whether you want to learn to ride to compete or simply enjoy the countryside from the back of a horse, riding can be enjoyed by all the family.

People from all walks of life can benefit from spending time with horses.

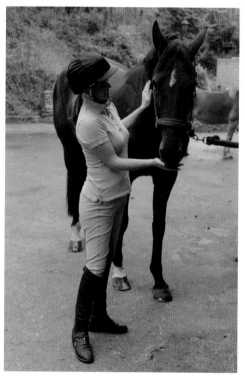

start riding as soon as they can walk, but many start in later life and enjoy it just as much. Being around like-minded horse-lovers, people often form lifelong friendships too and there will always be someone to talk to about horses.

Riding is also very good for you physically. Research has shown that riding can expend sufficient energy to be classed as moderate-intensity exercise, which, if carried out for 150 minutes a week, is said to keep you healthy. In terms of calories, hacking out burns approximately 240 calories per hour, schooling a horse burns up to 360 calories per hour, while mucking out burns up to 80 calories per 10 minutes. Horse riding strengthens all your core body muscles, tones the all-important tum and bum areas and provides a relaxing cardiovascular workout.

Physical exercise also promotes well-being benefits linked to changes in mood, anxiety levels and self-esteem.

Riding is also a great form of exercise for people with various disabilities. For forty years, the Riding for the Disabled Association (RDA) has provided a form of therapy and enjoyment to people with disabilities all over the UK. A network of over 500 volunteer groups organise activities such as riding, carriage driving, vaulting and showjumping for up to 28,000 people each year.

Para equestrianism, governed by the International Federation for Equestrian Sports (FEI), enables disabled people to compete in equestrian sports such as para-dressage, at international level, including participation in the Paralympics.

Riding can be used to mentally and physically stimulate disabled people and help enhance their lives through improved balance and coordination, increased self-confidence and a feeling of freedom and independence.

Hippotherapy utilises the horse's movement to improve a person's cognitive ability, coordination, balance and fine motor skills. Horses also pro-vide psychological benefits in the form of equine-assisted or equine facilitated therapy to those who suffer from mental disorders such as anxiety, mood swings and behavioural problems.

Recent initiatives

Hoof is the British Equestrian Federation's (BEF) Olympic and Paralympic legacy campaign set up after the London 2012 Olympic Games, which aims to encourage more people to take up horse-riding, driving, vaulting and volunteering. By introducing people to riding centres, schools, clubs and equestrian sporting organisations, Hoof is helping more people to discover horses, get fit and improve their well-being.

Trot to be Trim is a new health and fitness campaign organised by the BEF to promote the many health benefits associated with riding and being involved in horses.

For more information on both these topics, visit: www.hoofride.co.uk

History of the horse

Horses have played an important role throughout human history all over the world, both in warfare and in peaceful pursuits such as transportation, trade and agriculture. Without them, our lives would be very different.

It is believed that horses were first ridden approximately 4500 BC, although they were possibly domesticated much earlier when there were significant moves among many peoples from a hunter-gatherer lifestyle towards farming and raising of herds of animals. For instance, during the Neolithic era in Eurasia, around 4000 BC, there was such a shift, when mankind moved away from wholesale hunter-gathering, realising the advantages of domesticating herd animals as a ready source of meat.

Although domestication of various animals was originally carried out to provide a ready food source, it soon became apparent to humans that some species had other uses as pack and draught animals – horses in particular were seen to be readily trainable and could be used to help with the heavy work involved in farming.

It was from this point, taming horses for work on the farm, that humans learned they could sit astride a horse to assist with control, and this led to a completely different use for the horse – travel.

In the beginning, riders would cling to their horses, but there was little finesse in terms of dictating speed and direction, so forms of saddle and bridle were invented to help with these issues and make it easier to stay on. Excavations around the Black Sea area have unearthed examples of simple bridles from this era – these were nothing more than sinew placed around the horse's nose or rawhide hooked round the lower part of the horse's jaw.

Once able to exercise basic control, people from this region were able to migrate readily, with many moving southwards to more fertile areas in the Near East. While there is some evidence to suggest horses were ridden before they were driven, there are chariot burials in the Southern Urals, circa 2000 BC, so by the middle of the second millennium BC, in addition to being ridden in the Near East, horses were pulling chariots in Greece, Egypt, Mesopotamia and China. At this stage, horsemanship developed further and took on new roles to train horses for use in warfare and hunting. From as early as 1500 BC, horses were being used as powerful tools by armies. In the Near East and the Mediterranean the horse's strength, speed and stamina were used to conquer nations.

The Egyptians and the Anatolians were the great builders of empires and were also known for their great horsemanship – the Anatolian horseman is well-documented for training horses for battle. He selected horses who were healthy and fit and developed specific feeding plans for them. He also understood the horse's mind and how horses think and his methods are still seen in horsemanship around the world today.

Breed development

As with many domesticated animals, horses began to develop into types and breeds. Environmental factors such as temperature and soil type had an impact on how this happened in different parts of the globe.

The fourth and fifth centuries AD saw various Asian tribes invade western Asia and these warriors soon came across the desert tribes with their hot-blooded Arabian horses. These horses were well suited to travelling long distances in the hot, arid conditions of the desert. They were and still are known for their speed, agility, beauty and sensitivity.

In the Middle Ages, the need arose for bigger, more powerful horses to carry knights in full armour as well as wearing their own armour. These horses were developed from the bigger, more docile cold-blooded types originating from the colder European countries.

By the fifteenth century, the need for heavy armour was fading and with it, the use of giant cold-blooded horses on the battlefield, where smaller, lighter-framed, speedier horses replaced them.

These giant horses weren't forgotten however and soon became used for heavy draught work, their strength and willing nature making them suitable for working unforgiving terrain and pulling heavy loads on rough roads. In contrast, the use of the lighter breeds was expanded for riding and lighter driving and they were selectively bred for speed, agility and beauty.

Pony breeds, too, were utilised for a variety of jobs from pulling vehicles to pack work and riding.

Nowadays, there are now over 400 horse and pony breeds across the globe, each with their own roles to play.

Sport horses

Horse racing has been a sport of nearly every major civilisation since records began. Some records show that nomadic tribesmen in Asia raced horses very soon after it is thought that they were first ridden (in the fifth millennium BC) and by 638 BC the ancient Greeks had added chariot racing and mounted horse racing to the events in the Olympic Games.

During the twelfth century AD, English knights returned from North Africa and the Near East with hot-blooded horses and by the seventeenth

Point-to-point is a form of racing where horses race around a course of brush fences.

century, horse racing was popular with English gentry. Charles II soon learned that these hot-blooded horses could improve his stock and the resulting offspring had both speed and stamina.

In recent centuries, the horse's role has changed immensely and although some older cultures and less developed countries still rely heavily on horsepower for survival, in more developed countries nowadays horses tend only to be used for farm work or transportation by those enthusiasts who wish to retain or promote traditional practices.

Generally, horses are used for pleasure and competition in a variety of disciplines. While equestrian sport began with racing, our modern-day horse sports have various historic roots – polo, for example, is believed to have been played in some form as long ago as 500 BC in the reign of the Persian King Darius, although it was not introduced into Europe until 1869 when British officers brought it back from India.

Many early sports were rooted in military requirements. Dressage, which means 'training' in French, had its origins in developing movements for use on the battlefield. During the Renaissance, these movements were developed and refined in an artistic manner, with horses being taught to execute great leaps and manoeuvres in what was called *haute école* (high school).

Another sport to develop out of military training was three-day eventing. This sport originally included dressage, a 'speed and endurance' phase with a steeplechase section, cross-country and showjumping, testing a horse's accuracy, speed, stamina and endurance over three days. Eventing, also known as 'horse trials', has subsequently been refined into three, two and one-day forms, with the 'speed and endurance' phase having been discontinued at top level in recent years.

Jumping horses became prevalent in Britain following enforcement of the Enclosure Act in the eighteenth century, which meant that riders (particularly those engaged in hunting) had to jump fences to take the shortest route on their journeys. For a long time, riders would lean backwards over fences, as seen in many old hunting prints, and this was also the method taught by many military schools. One of the people most influential in changing this practice was the Italian instructor, Federico Caprilli, who promoted what became known as the forward seat. The early years of the twentieth century saw the development of the sport of showjumping, in which horses jump over a course of obstacles made up of coloured poles, planks, etc., set in wings. The first international horse show was staged at Olympia in 1907: most participants at this show, and other early shows, were of military background, but it was not long before the sport attracted civilian competitors.

Polo was introduced to Britain in 1869 when British officers brought it back from India.

Dressage is based on early military training and requires a strong bond between horse and rider.

below Eventing involves dressage, showjumping and cross-country.

The modern Olympic era began in 1896. In 1900, the games included an individual jumping competition, but the next games which included an equestrian element were 1912. Nowadays, the Olympic equestrian sports include dressage, showjumping and three-day eventing.

Showjumping is also a separate sport in its own right.

Besides competitive sport, horses are also used for other recreational purposes such as pleasure riding and, as mentioned earlier, as both psychological and physical therapy.

INTERESTING FACTS › THE THOROUGHBRED

A breed famous for its speed and stamina on the racetrack, all Thoroughbreds can be traced back to three stallions brought to England in the seventeenth and early eighteenth centuries – the Darley Arabian, the Byerley Turk and the Godolphin Barb.

INTERESTING FACTS > UK'S RICHEST HORSE RACE

The Derby is Britain's richest horse race and the most prestigious Group 1 flat race. It is run at Epsom Downs in Surrey over a distance of one mile, four furlongs and 10 yards (2,423m), and is held in June every year. It is one of Britain's great national events and has a huge worldwide TV audience.

INTERESTING FACTS > THREE-DAY EVENTING

Badminton Horse Trials is one of the world's toughest cross-country courses and takes places in May each year in the park of Badminton House, the home of the Duke of Beaufort in Gloucestershire.

First held in 1949, the event attracts visitors from all over the world, with cross-country day seeing crowds of up to a quarter of a million – the largest for any paid-entry sport in the UK and the second in the world after the Kentucky Three-Day event held in Lexington, USA.

INTERESTING FACTS > PUISSANCE

The puissance is the high-jump competition in the world of showjumping and sees horses jumping a short course that includes a wall sometimes well over 2m in height. The current record is 2.40m held by German rider Franke Sloothaak. Riders have to go clear in each round in order to qualify for the next and the wall increases in height every round. The last rider or riders to clear the wall, win the competition. Two of the biggest puissance competitions in the UK are those held at the Horse of the Year Show at the NEC Birmingham and at Olympia in London every year.

CHAPTER ONE

WHERE TO RIDE

Approvals and licensing

Horse riding is a rewarding sport that can be enjoyed by all ages. However, it can sometimes be confusing picking the right riding school at which to learn.

All riding schools must, by law, hold a licence to operate their business under the Riding Establishments Acts 1964, 1970. The licence is granted by Local Authorities.

Other than the legal necessity to hold a licence (and public and employers' liability insurance), riding schools may be inspected and approved by one of two bodies (sometimes both). These are the Association of British Riding Schools (ABRS) and the British Horse Society (BHS). Approved establishments serve all sections of the riding public, whether they ride for pleasure or have more serious aspirations, such as a career with horses or to compete.

The ABRS is the only organisation solely representing professional riding school proprietors. It conducts national approval schemes, setting a high standard for horse care and ensuring that the instruction given is well presented and correct in content. At an ABRS approved school, clients should receive sound instruction on suitable horses and ponies using good, safe and well-kept saddlery. Current member schools are listed on the ABRS website (www.abrs-info.org) and more information is available from the ABRS office.

The BHS also holds a list of approved establishments that have been inspected by a highly experienced representative of the BHS. They will have carefully inspected the level of instruction available to clients, the on-site facilities and equipment, and the standards of safety, horse care and management. The BHS website www.bhs.org.uk provides further information, including a list of over 600 approved riding establishments across the UK and Ireland, ensuring that wherever you live, there will be an approved establishment not too far away.

Personal research

Choosing an approved riding school should ensure that it is safe and well run, but word of mouth recommendation may also be useful and there's no better way of getting to know a place than by visiting it and judging for yourself.

When visiting a riding school, take some time to look at the following:

- Does the school have a variety of horses to cater for the types of rider they specialise in teaching – such as steady horses and ponies for beginner riders?

- Do the horses and other riders seem happy and content?

- Is the tack and equipment in a good, clean condition?

- Are the riding areas safe and properly enclosed, with well maintained surfaces?

- Is the atmosphere friendly, with patient and knowledgeable instructors offering a good standard of instruction?

- Do the instructors have the correct qualifications to teach beginners?

Although, as a beginner, you will not be in a position to evaluate the finer points of instruction, watching a lesson at a riding centre will give you a useful overview of how good the horses and instructors are. The general demeanour of the pupils may also give a useful insight with regard to 'customer satisfaction'.

above Riding arenas should have well-secured boundaries and flat, smooth surfaces that are well-maintained.

When choosing a riding centre, ensure that the horses look happy and content.

A clean, tidy stable yard with happy, healthy horses.

What to look for in an instructor

Finding the right instructor to suit you is a very personal thing. Everyone learns differently and while some prefer a strict, more direct instructor who gets results quickly, others would rather learn from someone less pushy who takes their time.

Qualifications are important, and the BHS train people to become instructors using a tiered training scheme. On their website you can find a list of instructors in your area, qualified to various standards that will suit your level of experience.

When first learning to ride, choose someone who is friendly, with a clear voice, who is approachable and happy to answer any questions you may have. A confident person will know how to deal with certain situations whilst also making your lessons fun so that you learn lots.

A good way to start is by asking at your local riding school for recommendations. If you decide that you might not, or don't, get along with a certain person, you can always try someone else. You want your riding lessons to be an enjoyable experience, so make sure you get on well with your instructor.

Check that your instructor has the correct qualifications and insurance.

CHAPTER TWO

WHAT TO WEAR

Being safe and comfortable are the most important things when learning to ride, and it all starts with your head.

Hard hat

It's vitally important that you wear a correctly fitting hat that meets approved safety standards. Riding can be dangerous and your instructor will not allow you to ride unless you are wearing an approved hat.

All hats should carry a safety certificate inside and the current standards are EN1384:1996 with CE mark, BSEN1384:1997 with CE mark, PAS015:2011 with BSI Kitemark, ASTM F1163:2004a with SEI mark, E2001 with Snell certification label and AS/NZ 3838:2006 with SAI global mark.

The CE mark means that the hats comply with the regulations implementing the European Community directive 89.686EC (Statutory Instrument 1992 no: 3139).

Hats should also ideally be Kitemarked. The Kitemark is a quality assurance mark and is the registered trademark of the British Standards Institute (BSI). It can only be affixed to products certified by them. BSI Kitemarked hats to the European Standard are stamped BS EN 1384. The Kitemark shows that helmets are independently and regularly batch-tested by the BSI to the appropriate specification. Hats tested elsewhere in the European Union may be tested to the EN 1384 standard. However, they will not carry the BSI Kitemark that is strongly recommended by the BHS and many insurance companies.

There are lots of different styles of riding hat, but as long as the hat you choose meets the safety standards, the design you opt for is up to you. However, when buying a hat, never buy one second-hand and always buy from a reputable equestrian retailer. It is important that the hat fits properly and therefore it should be fitted by a suitably qualified person, who

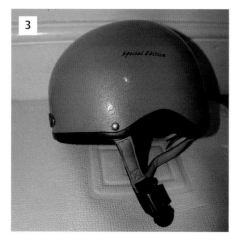

1 A lightweight, breathable riding hat.

2 A velvet-covered riding hat, with harness.

3 A skull cap.

4 Skull cap with coloured silk.

5 Kite mark inside a riding hat.

has been trained to do this and has British Equestrian Trade Association (BETA) approval. Most tack shops will have such a member of staff.

It's always best to acquire your own hat as soon as possible, but don't worry if you haven't at first because most schools have hats that you can use when you go for your initial lesson. However, check with them when first booking. Any hat loaned by a school should be in a condition to provide suitable protection otherwise, in the event of a head injury, the school might be liable for negligence.

Riding hats can only offer the optimum level of protection if they are undamaged. If you have a fall, the hat may not show any damage obvious to the naked eye but it could need replacing. If your hat has any deep cracks, obvious damage to the outer surface, thinning of the lining, or it creaks and gives when you push two sides together, it definitely needs replacing.

This rider is wearing a body protector and correctly fitted riding hat.

Body protectors

Body protectors are another recommended piece of safety kit. They will offer protection to your back and ribs if you have a fall. There are three levels of protection available which have been assessed by BETA: BETA level 1 (black label) for jockeys only; BETA level 2 (brown label) for basic needs; and BETA level three for normal riding, jumping and working with horses. As with hats, it's important that you get your body protector fitted correctly to ensure maximum protection. Body protectors are mandatory when riding across country and some riding schools will request you wear one when jumping or hacking out.

Air jackets are inflatable vests worn by the rider; they are attached by a cord to the front of the saddle. When a rider is unseated or thrown from a horse, the cord is pulled, which inflates the air vest to absorb shock, distribute pressure and support a rider's spinal column. When inflated, the airbag system offers the collar of the neck and trunk more support, therefore reducing the risk of over-bending the spinal column. Air jackets are often used for higher-levels sports such as eventing, and the recommendation is that they are worn with a traditional body protector for optimum protection, but they can be worn alone by riders having lessons or hacking out and we have seen a few novice riders use them in this way as they are less bulky than normal body protectors. The only concern is that the noise when the air canister goes off can really spook the horse. If you are considering wearing one of these, it might be an idea to check the riding centre's view on them.

Check that your body protector is the correct safety level and has the certification marks as seen here.

Air jackets inflate when you fall and help protect your spine and neck.

above Air jackets are attached to a canister which inflates when the rider leaves the saddle. The canister is attached to the saddle via a cord as see here.

Footwear

When choosing footwear, long riding boots or jodhpur boots with half-chaps or gaiters are ideal but a strong pair of boots that cover the ankle and have a smooth sole and heel will suffice. A boot with a high ankle will protect you from stirrup rubs and a small heel will stop your foot from slipping through the stirrup iron. Trainers should not be worn as they offer little protection (either when riding or if your foot is trodden on) and they can easily become stuck in the stirrup as they are wide, have a ridged sole and have no heel. Wellington boots are also not recommended as they do not have a smooth sole and can also get stuck in the stirrup because they are likely to be a little wide.

Completely unacceptable footwear includes flip-flops, sandals, open-toe shoes, shoes with heels higher than a couple of centimetres, or with no heel at all, such as pumps.

This rider is wearing jodhpur boots and leather gaiters, and riding with shortened stirrup leathers, as for jumping.

Other clothing

Jodhpurs are very comfortable trousers des-igned specifically for riding, but for beginner riders, a pair of strong trousers without a seam on the inside leg and not too bulky in the crotch area will be fine. Trousers that are very loose will tend to move up and down your leg during riding and can cause rubs on your skin – tighter-fitted trousers or leggings are more suitable. Tracksuit trousers can also be fairly comfortable when you are starting out.

Neither shorts nor three-quarter length trousers are advisable as they will not protect your skin should you fall off, and shorts offer no protection to the lower legs when riding.

For reasons of protection, vest tops are not advisable. It is preferable to wear a long-sleeved shirt, or a sweatshirt or fastened jacket (depending on weather conditions) to keep you comfortably warm and to protect your arms. Since riding is predominantly an outdoor sport it is always necessary to dress for the weather. A warm, waterproof coat is essential in winter, as is sun cream in the summer months.

More or less regardless of the weather, it's also advisable to wear a pair of riding gloves. In addition to helping prevent blisters when first

Leggings such as those pictured and a long-sleeved top are suitable for your first riding lessons.

learning to ride, these can keep your hands acceptably warm in cold weather, and assist your hold on the reins in wet weather, or if the horse gets sweaty on his neck. They are available in various patterns, but over-thick gloves are to be avoided as they reduce your 'feel' on the reins.

It is also advisable not to wear jewellery that could get caught up in anything, such as hoop earrings, rings or long chains and necklaces.

Finally, it may be worth asking whether the riding centre you choose has any particular views on dress and to comply with any guidance they have to offer.

CHAPTER THREE

HORSES – WHAT YOU NEED TO KNOW

Horse and pony colours and markings

Coat colours

Not only do horses and ponies come in a variety of heights and shapes, but they also boast a wide range of different colours. The most common are:

Black – completely black all over the body including the mane and tail.

Bay – reddish-brown body and head with black mane, tail and lower legs.

Brown – brown hairs that may vary in shade.

Chestnut – this colour comes in a variety of shades including copper and reddish-brown. The mane and tail may be a lighter, more flaxen, shade than the coat.

Palomino – golden coloured coat with white or cream mane and tail.

Roan – white hairs mixed with black (blue roan), bay (red roan) or chestnut (strawberry roan).

Grey – varies from white to dark grey including a variety of shades such as dappled and flea-bitten. A grey coat usually lightens with age, and many horses who are distinctly grey when young look almost white as they become older.

Piebald and skewbald – a piebald has large, irregular patches of white and black; a skewbald has large, irregular patches of white and any other colour except black.

Spotted – as its name suggests, the horse has dark spots over his body.

Dun – sandy-coloured body with black legs, mane and tail. Some also have a black stripe that runs along their spine, called a dorsal stripe.

Face and leg markings

Snip – a narrow white mark between the nostrils.

Stripe – a thin white mark down the horse's face.

Blaze – a wide white mark down the front of the horse's face.

Star – a small splodge of white on the horse's forehead.

Stocking – white extending from the hoof to the knee or hock.

Sock – white extending from the hoof to the fetlock joint.

Ermine – small black patches around the coronet band on a white sock.

Snip   Stripe   Blaze   Star

Common face markings.

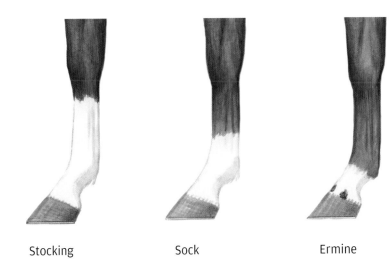

Common leg markings.

Stocking   Sock   Ermine

INTERESTING FACTS > THE NATURAL HORSE

Horses are prey animals so their first reaction to a threat is to run away, although if there is no other choice, they will stand their ground and defend themselves, especially if they are protecting their young.

Horses are herd animals and very sociable, with a clear herd pecking order, usually led by a dominant mare. This mare will keep the younger horses in check, lead the herd to water and tell them when it's time to stop for rest. She will be on the lookout for predators and other horses who threaten the herd.

INTERESTING FACTS > SLEEP

Horses are able to sleep both standing up and lying down. They have special leg adaptations (called the stay apparatus)which allow their legs to lock into place and stop them falling over when they sleep.

Horses in the open sleep better when in groups because some animals will sleep while others stand guard to watch for predators. Horses sleep in short periods of about 15minutes at a time throughout the day and get about three hours of sleep a day in total.

Horse body language

Although horses communicate by using their voices, they do so mainly through body language – they use certain movements or gestures to communicate how they feel. It's important to understand these signs so that you know how to act according to the horse's body language.

Ears back and eyes shut with a hind leg resting – this horse is asleep or dozing. You need to talk to him to waken him and only approach when his eyes are open and he has turned his head to look at you with his ears pricked forwards.

Ears flat back – he is angry and may bite or kick out. This facial expression is normally an aggressive one to scare other horses and humans if he is being protective over his space, food or another horse. You should be careful when approaching a horse like this.

Ears back – some horses can have their ears back because they are listening to what is happening behind them, but it doesn't mean they are being aggressive. However, only approach a horse like this if an experienced person is with you or the horse changes his ears to a forward position so you are sure he is paying attention to you.

Ears sideways – he is relaxed so you will need to talk to him to get his attention before approaching.

One ear forward and one back – he is trying to listen to where a sound is coming from.

Both ears forward – he is focused on a noise or object.

Swishing tail – this could be simply flicking a fly away, but horses can also swish their tails continually and more vigorously if something is irritating them or they are upset.

Head held high – horses will hold their heads up high if they are alert to something and are looking up into the distance. It could mean that they are about to take flight.

Resting a hind leg – this usually means that the horse is relaxed, but if he is holding his hind leg a little way above the ground, it could mean that he is about to kick out (or possibly be lame in a hind leg).

Head down – the horse can sometimes droop his head low to the floor if he is sleeping, or if he is feeling unwell.

The senses

Because horses are prey animals, they must be aware of their surroundings at all times and on the lookout for danger. They have the largest eyes of any land mammal, and excellent day and night vision. Their eyes are positioned on the sides of their heads, rather than at the front like humans, and this means that horses have a range of vision of more than 350 degrees. However, they do have two 'blind spots' (areas where the animal cannot see). These are directly in front of the face and right behind the head, an area that extends over the back and behind the tail. That is why you are often told never to stand directly behind a horse, because he cannot see you.

A horse's hearing is also good, and each ear can rotate up to 180 degrees, which means that the horse has the potential for hearing sounds coming from any direction without having to move his head (although he will often do so, and prick his ears towards any sound that particularly attracts his attention). Noise can affect the behaviour of horses and they can find certain noises very stressful. People often leave the radio on for stabled horses and research has shown that horses prefer country or classical music, rather than jazz or rock music. It is interesting that horses trained to do dressage to music often learn to associate the progression of the music to the movements they have been trained to do to it.

above left This horse's ears are back but not flat on his head, which means he is relaxed and not paying attention to anything in particular.

above centre Eyes closed and ears back usually means the horse is relaxed and possibly asleep.

above right Ears forwards show the horse is concentrating on something ahead of him.

In their natural habitat, it would be dangerous for horses to lose their balance and they have a great sense of balance enhanced by their ability to feel their footing and by their highly developed proprioception (the unconscious sense of where the body and limbs are at all times).

The sense of touch is also well developed. The most sensitive areas are around the eyes, ears and nose, where horses have long whiskers to help them feel their way in the dark. Horses can sense the lightest of contact such as a fly landing on their body.

Their sense of smell is much better than that of humans and they have an advanced sense of taste and are able sort through the smallest pieces of food and pick out what they would most like to eat.

INTERESTING FACTS >
WHAT SCARES HORSES AND PONIES?

With their instinctive need to react quickly to things that might represent a threat, horses and ponies may exhibit fright in response to:

- loud and sudden noises
- things that move suddenly
- an unannounced approach from behind
- being touched if they are asleep/unaware of you
- objects they may not have seen before – such as an umbrella or a different coloured jump in the arena
- being trapped in a small space.

Points of the horse

This is the name traditionally given to key anatomical features. Key 'points' are shown in the photos opposite.

The horse is designed for speed and agility to be able to flee from predators. As a species, horses are the seventh fastest land mammals in the world, and have long legs and small feet. Their legs are shaped specifically to cover the ground quickly.

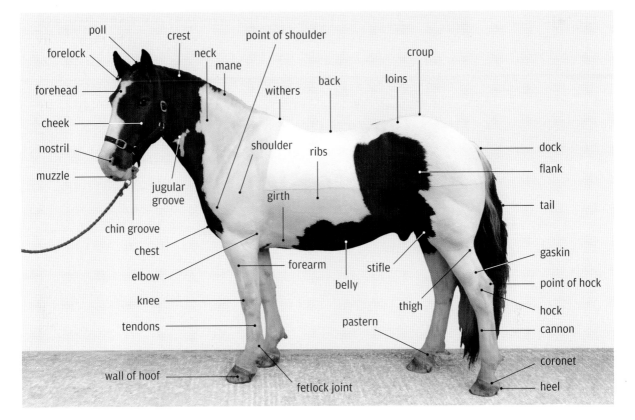

poll
forelock
crest
neck
mane
point of shoulder
forehead
back
croup
loins
cheek
withers
nostril
muzzle
shoulder
ribs
dock
flank
jugular groove
tail
chin groove
girth
chest
elbow
forearm
belly
stifle
gaskin
point of hock
knee
thigh
hock
tendons
pastern
cannon
wall of hoof
fetlock joint
coronet
heel

Points of the horse.

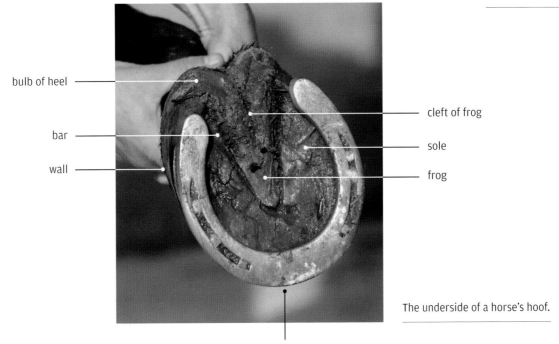

bulb of heel
bar
wall
cleft of frog
sole
frog
toe

The underside of a horse's hoof.

Some parts of the horse have strange names such as:

Frog – located on the underside of the horse's hoof, the frog is triangular in shape, assists grip and acts as a shock absorber for the hoof.

Wall – the protective shield covering the sensitive internal hoof tissues.

Chestnut –a callous-type growth located just above the knee or hock joint on the inside of the horse's leg; the remnants of a toe that the horse's ancestors are believed to have had.

Whorl – a circular patch of hair.

Dock – the muscle and skin covering the coccygeal vertebrae at the top of the horse's tail.

Feathers – long hairs found on lower legs of some breeds of horses, usually the heavier breeds, such as Shires.

Poll – bony lump found between the horse's ears.

Measuring horses

The height of horses is measured at the highest point of the withers, where the neck meets the back. This point is used because it is a stable point of the anatomy, unlike the head or neck, which move up and down in relation to the horse's body.

The English-speaking world has traditionally measured the height of horses in hands and inches: one hand is equal to 4 inches.

The height is expressed as the number of full hands, followed by a point, then the number of additional inches, ending with the abbreviation 'h' or 'hh' (for 'hands high'). So, a horse described as '15.2 hh' is 15 hands plus 2 inches, for a total of 62 inches (157.5 cm) in height.

Some breed and showing societies have, in recent years, adopted standard metric measurement for horses and ponies, rather than using the traditional system.

Gaits

Most horses have four basic gaits: the four-beat walk, which averages 4mph; the two-beat trot at 8–12mph; the canter, a three-beat gait that is 12–15mph; and the gallop, which is the fastest gait. Potential gallop speeds vary according to the horse's breed, type and fitness, but for 'average' horses it will be in the region of 25 mph. Racehorses can gallop substantially faster than this and flat-racing Thoroughbreds are sometimes clocked at speeds in excess of 40mph.

Walk

This is the slowest gait of the horse and has a four-beat rhythm. It is the gait that horses normally use to move around when they are in their natural wild habitat or when they are grazing in the field.

The sequence of the walk. The photos below show it starting with the left hind leg, but it can also start with the right hind.

1 Starting with the left hind.

2 Followed by the left fore.

3 Then the right hind.

4 And finally the right fore.

INTERESTING FACTS › PHYSIOLOGY

- The structure of the horse's lower forelimb approximates to the human finger, and that of his hind limb to the human toe. This means that his hooves are like 'fingernails' and 'toenails' and he effectively runs along on his 'fingertips and tiptoes'.

- Like human fingernails, the horse's hooves grow continually and, in the wild, horses wear them down naturally from travelling across open plains on a daily basis, but domesticated horses need to have their feet trimmed or, in circumstances where they are ridden daily on hard surfaces, they will need metal shoes to protect their feet.

When walking the horse will have one foot off the floor and the other three on the ground at any particular moment. The sequence of legs as they are placed forwards and onto the ground is: the hind leg on one side, the foreleg on the same side, the hind leg on the other side, the foreleg on that side, e.g. if starting on the left – left hind, left fore, right hind, right fore.

Trot

Trot is an easy gait for the horse to use. In the wild it can be used to cover long distances without the horse becoming too tired.

Trot is a two-beat gait. The horse's legs move in diagonal pairs, e.g. left hind and right fore as a pair and then right hind and left fore as a pair. Between the footfalls of these diagonal pairs, there is a brief moment of 'suspension', when all four feet are off the ground.

Canter

Canter is a three-beat gait. Unlike walk and trot, it has a specific sequence of legs depending on which direction the horse is travelling in. When cantering clockwise ('on the right rein'), the sequence of footfalls is left hind, a diagonal pair of right hind and left fore, right fore and a moment of suspension. When cantering anticlockwise ('on the left rein'),

above, right and left In the trot, the horse's legs move in diagonal pairs.

1 Right fore and left hind diagonal pair.

2 Left fore and right hind diagonal pair.

sequence below The sequence of legs at canter.

1 Starts with the outside hind leg (in this case, the right hind).

2 Followed by the diagonal pair.

3 Then the leading foreleg (in this case, the left).

4 And then the moment of suspension.

the footfalls are right hind, a diagonal pair of left hind and right fore, left fore and a moment of suspension. Although the canter technically starts with the outside hind leg, it is the inside foreleg that is called the 'leading leg' and getting into canter is called 'striking off'. When your instructor wants you to go into canter clockwise, you will hear the instruction: 'Canter strike-off onto the right lead'. A canter strike-off onto the left lead will be when you are going anticlockwise.

It is possible for a horse to canter on one particular leading leg when going in the 'opposite direction' – i.e. to canter in left lead when going clockwise, or in right lead when going anticlockwise. This, when done deliberately, is called counter-canter: an experienced rider may do this on purpose as an exercise to help make the horse more supple, and it is a movement required in some dressage tests. When a rider has asked for the correct (normal, or 'true') canter lead but the horse picks up the opposite lead (i.e. counter-canters) as a result of not being asked correctly, or being unbalanced or less supple in one direction, this is referred to simply as being 'on the wrong leg'.

Because of the complex three-beat nature of canter, it is also possible for a horse to move his legs in an incorrect sequence, which is known as cantering 'disunited'.

Gallop

Gallop is the fourth natural gait of the horse. It is in some respects a faster version of canter (the French use the term *galop* for both gaits) but has a four-beat rhythm and also a moment of suspension. As with canter, the gallop has a 'leading leg', which is particularly significant if the horse is galloping on a curved line. It starts with the outside hind, then inside hind, then outside foreleg and lastly the inside foreleg, followed by a moment of suspension where all four feet are off the ground.

opposite page The sequence of legs at gallop.

1 Starts with the outside hind leg (in this case, the left).

2 Then the right hind.

3 Then the left fore.

4 Finally, the leading foreleg (in this case, the right).

5 Followed by the moment of suspension.

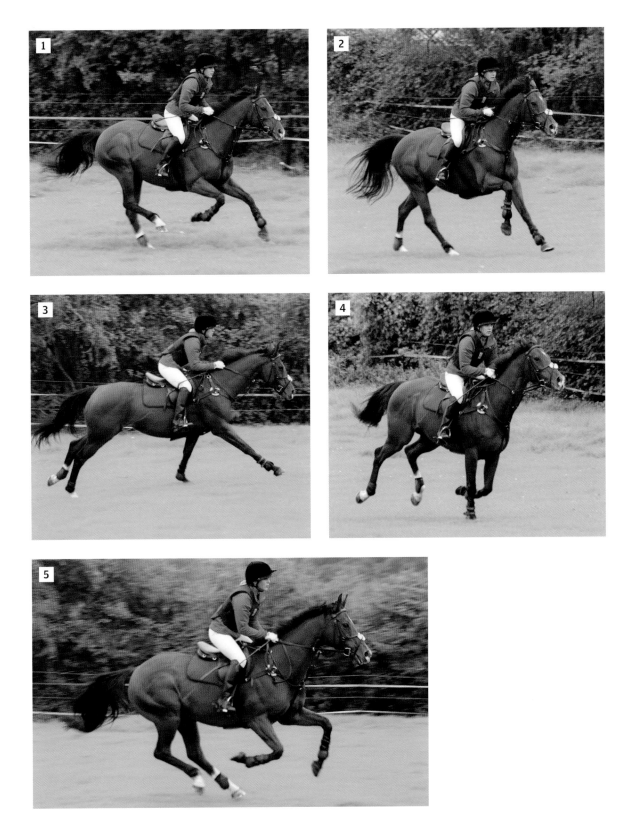

INTERESTING FACTS >

HORSE AND HUMAN HEART COMPARISONS

- The average adult horse's heart weighs around 3,500g (although some hearts – often associated with exceptional performance horses) can be twice as much. That's over ten times that of a human's heart, which weighs 250–300g.

- At rest, a human's heart beats on average 60–100 beats per minute (bpm). At walk, the rider's heart beats at around 75–90bpm, at trot 120bpm and at canter 140bpm. A horse's resting heart rate is around 30–50bpm, at walk 80bpm, at trot 120bpm and canter 180bpm. A galloping horse's heart rate can reach up to 220–240bpm.

CHAPTER **FOUR**

SADDLERY AND TACK

When learning to ride, it's important that you understand the equipment you are using as your instructor may refer to certain items of tack during your lessons.

You will sit on a saddle, which is usually made of leather, but also comes in synthetic materials. A saddle will have stirrup leathers and irons attached to either side, which you put your feet into, and it is attached to the horse using a girth, which is the strap that runs under the horse's belly.

Your reins (two long straps, usually of leather, but sometimes of material such as webbing) will be attached to the bridle, which is the assembly of leather on the horse's head. The bit is the piece of metal in the horse's mouth and this is what the reins attach to. The bit helps control your direction and speed.

During your initial lessons, your instructor will show you how to hold the reins correctly, check your girth to ensure that it is tight enough, and show you how to loosen it when your lesson has finished. You will also learn how to shorten and lengthen your stirrup leathers to the correct length for your legs and how to run the stirrups down before mounting and run them up when you have finished your lesson.

Saddles and stirrups

There are different types of saddle for different purposes, but you are likely to be riding in a general-purpose saddle when first learning. This type of saddle allows you to do all the riding activities including jumping and dressage to a certain level. For more specialist use, a dressage saddle is a different shape from a general-purpose saddle, with much longer, straighter flaps and a deeper seat. Jumping saddles are flatter in the seat area than general-purpose models, and the flaps are shorter and more shaped, with bigger knee rolls to help secure the rider when jumping.

You'll come across a variety of stirrup irons, including the Peacock which is a safety stirrup with the outer side designed to release if the foot becomes trapped in the stirrup; the bent iron which, as its name applies,

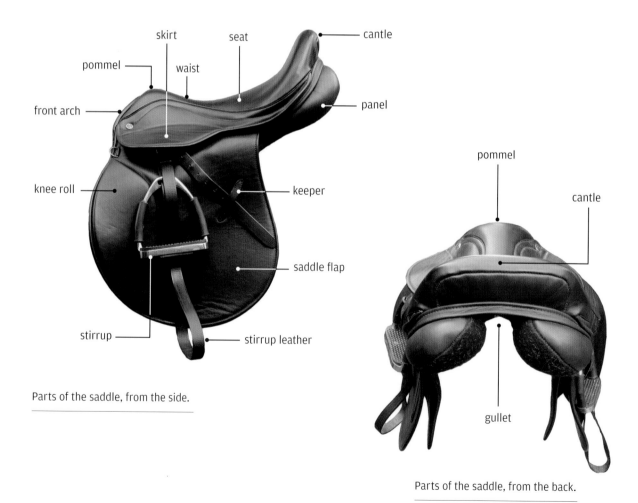

Parts of the saddle, from the side.

Parts of the saddle, from the back.

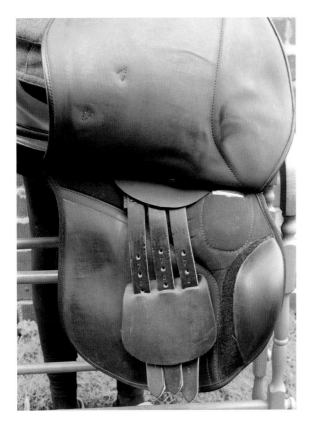

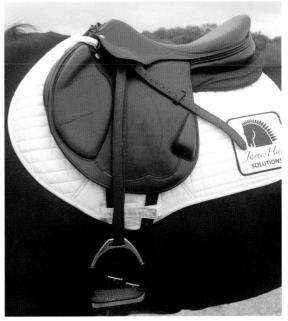

left Under the saddle flap, showing the girth straps.

above The jumping saddle has a much flatter seat and more shaped flaps than a dressage saddle.

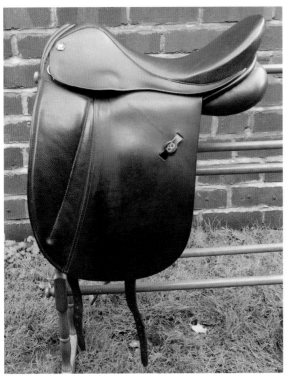

above A peacock stirrup showing the rubber safety band.

left A dressage saddle showing the straight flaps and deep seat.

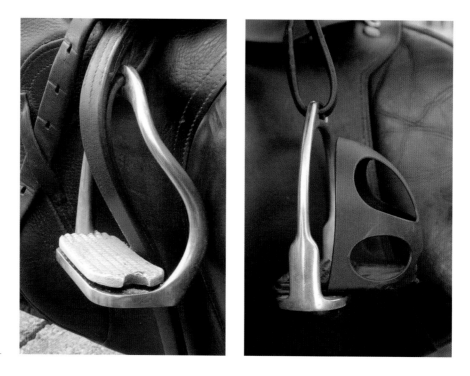

right Curved safety stirrup.

far right Closed-toe stirrup for endurance and long distance riding.

has a bent shape also to prevent the foot from getting trapped; a closed-toe stirrup which is usually made of a synthetic material and often used for long-distance riding and trekking to make it more comfortable for the foot and stop the foot slipping through; and the Fillis iron which is a standard iron with a slightly wider base for the foot to rest on.

Bridles and leatherwork

Bridles are commonly made from leather, but can come in a variety of synthetic materials too. The headpiece and throatlash are made from one piece of leather with a browband preventing it from slipping backwards. The cheekpieces attach to the headpiece and hold the bit onto the bridle. The noseband is usually a separate piece of leather that feeds up and over the horse's head under the headpiece. The reins attach to the bit.

There is a variety of different types of bit, all with different shapes and designs. Some bits give you more control if your horse is strong. The most basic bit is the snaffle.

There are also different types of noseband, some of which are designed to keep the horse's mouth closed, such as the flash, but the most common, basic noseband is the cavesson.

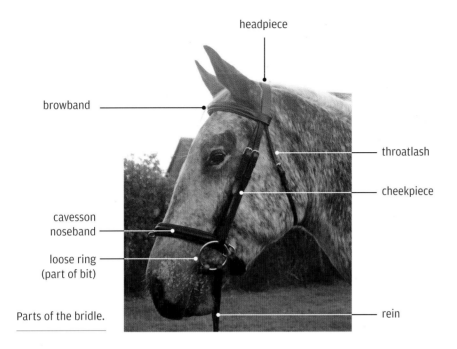

headpiece

browband

throatlash

cheekpiece

cavesson
noseband

loose ring
(part of bit)

Parts of the bridle.

rein

You may also come across a running martingale, which sits around the horse's neck and has a strap that attaches to the girth. The upper end of this strap divides into two, and rings are fitted to the divided sections, through which the reins pass. The purpose of this arrangement is to discourage the horse from lifting his head too high. A standing martingale (nowadays less common than the running version) is a straight piece of leather that attaches to the girth and runs up through the horse's forelegs to the underside of the noseband. It also stops the horse from getting his head too high.

A neckstrap is a simple piece of leather that sits around the horse's neck to give riders something to hold onto. A breastplate or breast girth is similar to the lower part of a martingale except it doesn't have rings for the reins to go through, but does have straps that attach to rings on the saddle. If a horse's conformation is such that the saddle might tend to slip backwards, a breastplate will help to keep it in place.

CHAPTER **FIVE**

MEETING HORSES AND HANDLING THEM

It can be an exciting and yet daunting prospect meeting a horse or pony for the first time, especially if you have not had contact with such a large and impressive animal before. It is a fascinating and enjoyable experience to be able to interact with a horse or pony as, despite their size, domesticated horses are friendly, gentle and interact well with humans.

Your first contact when you are learning to ride will normally be at a riding stable where the horses and ponies are specially selected for their temperament and calmness. It will be noticeable that the staff and other riders there may seem very comfortable handling the horses, but how do you start safely?

Horses and ponies have been domesticated for well over 6,000 years but while this may seem a long time, remember that the horse, in various ancestral forms, has been in existence for some 55 million years. While domesticated horses can be easily handled and ridden by humans, at heart the horse remains a creature of flight and his nature is to flee when frightened. When handling horses and being around them, remember that you need to be confident and calm and your voice and actions should replicate this.

It's very important to let horses know that you are there so that you don't startle them. As mentioned earlier, a horse can sleep standing up, so although you may think he is awake, he may actually be sleeping. So how do we let him know we are there without scaring him?

Every time you approach a horse, follow these steps:

- Look at his face to see if he has noticed you.

- Look at his ears – as mentioned earlier they are a big indicator of whether he has heard you, and also of his mood.

- Talk in a moderate and calm voice while you approach from the side. Walk confidently towards his shoulder and not towards his hindquarters.

- Touch him with a flat hand, using a firm but gentle pressure. Using one finger and being too gentle can tickle the horse and make him swish his tail or kick out as it can be mistaken for a fly. Also, touching him too hard can make him move away or overreact.

How to approach a horse correctly.

How to move round a horse safely

When being handled in the stable or on the yard, the horse must be tied up so it is safe to handle him. The lead rope is attached to a ring on the headcollar under the horse's chin by a clip. The other end of the rope is tied to a piece of breakable string (often known as baler twine, used to bale hay and straw) that is tied round a 'tie ring' secured to the wall. When the horse is tied up, you can safely go under his neck, but not his tummy. When moving under the horse's neck to go from one side to the other, it is best to hold the bridle or headcollar with one hand so the horse cannot cheekily nip you with his teeth when you are bending down. This will also keep control of his head and prevent him bumping his head with yours.

It's a common warning never to walk behind a horse, but it is quite safe as long as you do it correctly. When walking behind the horse, staying close to him is safer. This is because if the horse kicks out and you are in the way, believe it or not, it will be less painful if you are closer than if you are further away – the power created when the horse kicks out is greater when the leg is further away from his body. Remember that a lot of horses wear metal shoes and being in the way of a kicking or striking leg can be painful (as can having a horse stand on your foot). Never walk straight up behind a horse and touch him without warning.

When you walk behind a horse, make sure you keep your hand on him (without tickling or poking him) as you pass from one side to the other. This way, he always knows where you are. Always pay attention to the horse's reactions so that you are aware if he is suddenly spooked or about to kick. Horses respond well to the handler or rider talking to them so they are continually aware of where that person is, even if the person is in their blind spot.

When the horse is out of the stable and not tied up, and you need to do something like adjust the stirrups, it is only safe to go around his front end, unless you have a person to hold him so you can go around the back. To go around the front, you do not need to duck under the neck like you did when he was tied up. If he is wearing a bridle, use a gentle pressure on the reins to make him understand that when you go in front of his head, he needs to stay still and then you can move smoothly from one side around his head to the other. Make sure that, when you are the other side of him,

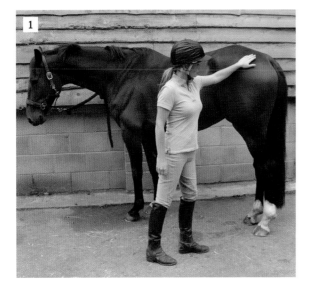

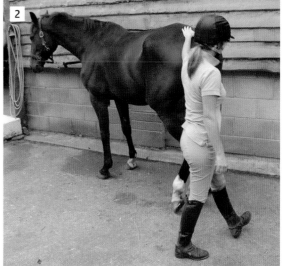

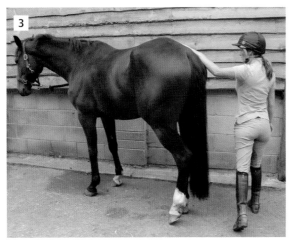

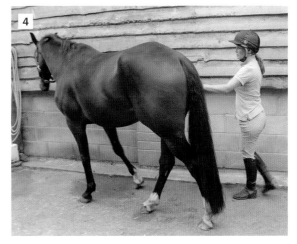

above How to move round behind a horse.

1 Place a hand on the horse's hindquarters.

2 Keep a hand on the horse.

3 Move slowly and stay close to the horse.

4 Talk to the horse as you move around him so he knows where you are.

right Never walk straight up behind a horse and pat him on the back without first letting him know you are there.

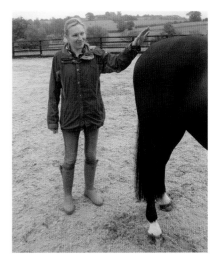

Dogs can frighten a horse so always approach facing the horse's head, not from behind him with a dog.

you swap the reins into the hand nearer to him to make it easier to keep control and prevent him moving, biting or pushing you with his head.

How to hold and lead a tacked-up horse

Most riding stables have helpers who bring the horses to the arena and help you put the horse away after your lesson – however, holding a horse and leading him will quickly be skills you need to master.

Holding a tacked-up horse

Make sure that, before you go into the stable, you have made the horse aware that you are going in by talking to him. When you are sure he is looking at you, walk up to his shoulder and pat his neck before sliding your hand up the neck to his head. Undo the headpiece of the headcollar using both hands and then hold the rein by the bit with your right hand while hooking the headcollar to the piece of string that the lead rope is attached to with your left hand.

Once this is done, you can use both hands to undo the throatlash to release the reins. The throatlash will then need to be done up so you can fit one hand's width between the strap and the horse's cheek. Or, if the reins have been secured behind the stirrups, you will need to take them out from under them. Once the reins are freed, take them carefully over the horse's head (unless he is wearing a martingale), making sure you do not catch them on his ears. Be careful not to let the reins hang close to the floor in case the horse walks forwards and accidentally treads on them. Sometimes you may find that the reins have been put round the horse's neck in a loop so, in this case, they need to be pulled over the horse's head and the throatlash will not need to be undone.

Now you can stand on the left-hand side of the horse and face forwards so your right shoulder is next to him. To ensure it is easy to control him, hold the reins with your right hand near to the bit but without pulling the

Releasing a tacked-up horse from the headcollar.

1 When taking the headcollar off, start by undoing the strap.

2 Then pass the strap over the horse's head.

3 Before slipping it off over his nose.

4 To release the reins from the throatlash, undo the throatlash, unravel the reins and then re-fasten the throatlash.

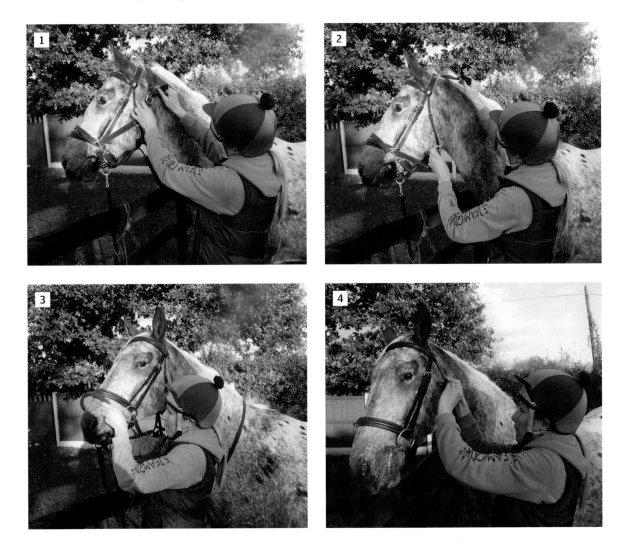

bit tight in his mouth; your left hand can hold the rest of the reins by the buckle where the two reins join together. This is the best way to hold a horse if you are waiting for your lesson or any other riding activity.

Leading a tacked-up horse

When you want to lead him, make sure you ask him with your voice: 'walk on' is the phrase to use. A gentle pull on the reins as you ask with the voice will make him start to move and then you need to walk with him. Speed can be controlled by a gentle voice saying 'steady' as well as using a gentle pressure on the reins near to the bit. Remember not to keep pulling at the bit or he may stop and refuse to move. When you are leading him, aim to stay parallel to his shoulder on his left-hand side as you were when he was standing still. You need to look forwards because staring directly at his face will make him back away. By walking parallel to him, you should not be in the way of his feet. If you need to turn him, always turn him to the right so you stay on the outside of the turn and remain in a safe position.

below left How to lead a horse correctly.

below right How not to lead a horse.

Looking directly at a horse and trying to drag him will frighten him and have the opposite effect to what you are trying to achieve.

That way, he can't tread on you because you are pushing him away from you, not pulling him toward you.

If the horse is tacked up with a martingale, then the reins are not brought over his head. You need to hold the rein with one hand close to the bit and lead the horse using just one hand, while making sure you do not step in the way of his feet.

Remember that, if you are carrying a whip, this will need to be in your left hand so it is not next to the horse as it may touch him accidentally. Also, note that the reins (or lead rope, if leading in a headcollar) must never be wrapped around your hand – if the horse pulls back, the loops will tighten around your hand and cause an injury. The stirrups need to be 'run up' the stirrup leathers so they do not bang on the horse's side or get caught on anything.

CHAPTER SIX

ARENAS, INSTRUCTOR'S PHRASES AND SCHOOL MOVEMENTS

At this point, you are probably keen to read on about the business of getting on and starting to ride, but it is worth spending a little time learning about the arena, and what the instructor's phrases mean in terms of moving around it.

Learning where the marker letters are will help you navigate around the arena – you can think of this a little like having driving lessons. If your driving instructor says 'Take the second turning right', you can prepare better if you know whether it is 40 yards or 400 yards ahead; similarly, if your riding instructor says 'Turn across the arena at H', it is useful to know whether you are on top of H, or right on the other side of the arena. Most of the movements used in the riding arena are geometrical patterns and, as you gain experience, these will become more complex, so being familiar with the layout of the arena will really help you to plan and ride them more accurately.

The phrases instructors use are mainly quite traditional, and they make sense once they have been explained, but there is an initial 'language barrier' to overcome. For example, 'closed order' doesn't refer to a secretive bunch of monks, and 'go large' is not an invitation to start binge eating.

The explanations given in this chapter are quite a lot to take in, and some will seem more relevant once you've had a little experience in the saddle, but you can always return to them for reference as and when required.

Layout of the arena

At your riding school, there will be an enclosed area with a sand or rubber-based surface which is called an arena.

Most arenas will be either 20 × 40m or 20 x 60m and they will have letters placed around them at measured-out positions on the fence or boundary (see the arena diagrams overleaf). These are used during dressage tests to show people where to perform specific movements and you will use them from day one when learning to ride. In a standard 20 × 40m arena, there are eight letters around the arena and in a 20 × 60m arena there are twelve. There are also 'invisible' letters along the centre line of the school, including X which marks the middle of the arena, and D and G which sit either side of X down the centre line. (In the 20 × 60m arena, there are also I and L markers on the centre line, but it is rare for these to be referred to in lessons for novice riders.)

The most common way of remembering all of the letters in a 20m × 40m arena, and the order in which they appear, is by saying this simple rhyme:

A – **A**ll

K – **K**ing

E – **E**dward's

H – **H**orses

C – **C**an

M – **M**anage

B – **B**ig

F – **F**ences

Arena marker.

A is situated in the middle of one end of the arena (and is where riders enter to start a dressage test), and C is in the middle of the other end.

A 20 × 60m arena uses the same letters as the smaller arena, but with extra letters in between: **A**, **K**, V, **E**, S, **H**, **C**, **M**, R, **B**, P, **F**. There is no mnemonic for this whole combination, but some people use the phrase Very Suddenly Refuse Poles to remember the four additional letters.

It is thought by some that these markers originated from a riding centre in Germany many years ago.

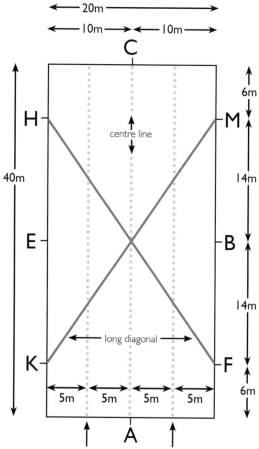

this is the quarter line when riding on the KH side of the arena and three-quarter line when riding on the MF side

this is the quarter line when riding on the MF side of the arena and three-quarter line when riding on the KH side

above Key lines in a 20 × 40m arena.

right Layout of a 20 × 60m arena.

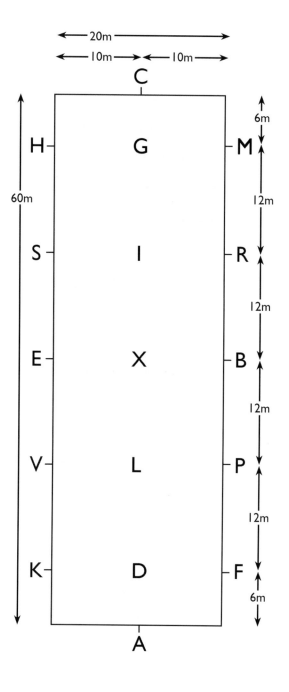

Instructor's references to the arena

Instructors will often mention areas of the arena in such terms such as:

The outside track – the outside edge of the arena.

Inner track – parallel to the outside track but 2 or 3m inside of it.

Centre line – the line down the centre from A to C, through X. It is 10m from both sides of the outer track.

Quarter and three-quarter lines – imaginary lines which run lengthwise in the arena, parallel to the centre line. These lines are both 5m from the centre line, and whether they are the 'quarter line' or the 'three-quarter line' depends upon the reference point (i.e. where you are when you refer to them). The quarter line is 5m in from the outside track nearest to it; the three-quarter line is 15m from the same track. For example, if you were riding along the outside track from K to H, the line 5m to your right would be the quarter line, and a line 5m away from the other side of the arena (and thus 15m from you) would be the three-quarter line. If you continued round the outside track of the arena and rode from M to F, what was previously your 'three-quarter line' would now be your 'quarter line', because it would now be 5m from you, and what was previously your 'quarter line' would now be your 'three-quarter line', because it would be 15m from you.

Long diagonal – a line from one of the letters near (but not in) one corner (see top tip below) of the arena, to the letter diagonally opposite; e.g. H to F, or K to M. Other diagonal lines can be ridden, but the long diagonals are the most common.

TOP TIPS › LETTER MARKERS K, H, M AND F

If you look at the arena diagrams, you will see that these letters are not actually in the corners of the arena; each is 6m away from the actual corner. When you are riding across the diagonal, it is important to ride from letter to letter, which will give you time and room to turn your horse properly. In particular, if you actually ride directly into a corner, your horse will not be able to turn through it correctly, maintaining energy and balance.

These four marker letters are correctly known as 'quarter markers' – not to be confused with the quarter line.

Understanding these references will help you to know where exactly in the arena to perform various movements and exercises. For example, a 5m loop or 15m circle can be ridden accurately if you know how far you need to ride out from the side of the arena.

Instructor's terms and phrases

There are a number of terms and phrases that are used by instructors to refer to particular aspects of riding, to tell pupils what to do and where to go. Some apply to both individual lessons and group lessons, others to group lessons only. The most common are:

As a ride/Whole ride – everyone is being asked to ride the same exercise. For example, 'As a ride change the rein' or 'Whole ride prepare to halt'.

Leading file – this describes the rider at the front of the ride.

Rear file – this is the rider at the back of the ride.

Closed order – riders follow behind one another, with one and a half horse's distance between their horse and the one in front.

Open order – the riders in the lesson are working individually and not following each other. When doing this you will need to be aware of where everyone else is and make sure you follow the school rules to avoid crashing into each other.

Go large – ride around the outside track of the arena. For example, if this is said when you are riding a circle at A, when you next arrive back at A you come off the circle and carry on round the arena on the outside track.

Track – although sometimes simply a reference to the outside track ('the track'), this can be used as a direction, for example:, if you were riding up the centre line towards C and your instructor said: 'At C track right', this means that when you reach the C marker, you should turn right onto the outside track.

Change the rein – this is an instruction to turn into the opposite direction – i.e. steer horse from one rein to the other. So, if you were on the left rein (going anticlockwise) then your instructor would be asking you to change onto the right rein (going clockwise). There are various ways to do this and, until you are more advanced and riding in open order (see above) the instructor will be specific in telling you where and how you are to turn. Three common ways of doing this are across the diagonal, down the centre line and across the school from E to B (or B to E). The full instruction would be, for example, 'At H, change the rein across the diagonal to F'.

Change your diagonal – if you change the rein in rising trot (see Chapter 9), you will need to change your diagonal, which means you will have to sit for an extra beat before resuming the up-down motion.

More general terms used in talking about lessons include:

Schooling – training the horse to perform certain movements and exercises.

Flat work – riding a horse on the flat, without jumps or poles being included.

Jumping – riding over obstacles.

Pole work – using poles on the ground for exercises such as regulating trot and canter.

Arena/school/manège – different terms used for the enclosed area with a synthetic surface where you have your lessons.

School movements

Every rider uses certain arena movements to learn how to ride and train their horse. Here are some key movements used in everyday riding.

Down the centre line. This can be ridden from A to C or from C to A. The turn starts from the corner before A or C and should be ridden as a 10m half-circle, starting just after the quarter marker (letter near the corner, see Top Tips page 59) and arriving onto the centre line straight. This is often used as a way of changing the rein.

Turn straight across the school from one letter to another. Any of the letters on opposite sides of the arena can be used, but most commonly E to B (or vice versa). This line can be used to change the rein and the turn at each letter is similar in shape to a rounded corner.

Riding down the centre line.

below Making a half-circle right back to the track from the centre line.

Across the diagonal. As mentioned above, using the long diagonal is another way of changing the rein and involves riding from K to M (or vice versa), passing X when crossing the middle of the school on the right rein, or F to H (or vice versa) on the left rein.

A 20m circle. In riding, circle sizes are always defined by their diameter. A 20m circle therefore covers the whole width of a standard arena. It can be started from various points in the arena but the most common starting points are at either end of the school at C or A and in the middle at E or B.

top Changing the rein across the school from E to B.

lower photo Completing the change of rein from E to B.

Changing the rein across
the diagonal from K to M.

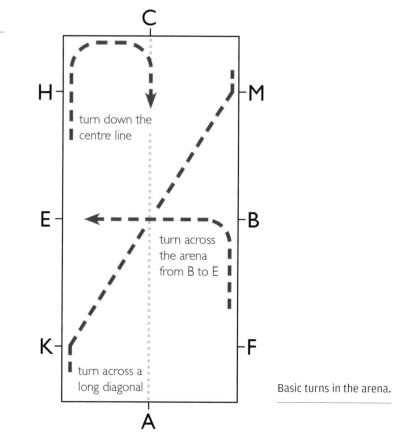

turn down the
centre line

turn across
the arena
from B to E

turn across a
long diagonal

Basic turns in the arena.

15 and 10m circles. The smaller a circle, the harder it is to ride so, when you begin, you will mainly ride 20m circles as just described. The next 'standard' circle size is 15m: this will help you become proficient in riding correct size and shape, both because it is a bit smaller, and because the reference points are less obvious than for a 20m circle. When you ride a 15m circle starting from a long side, the diameter extends to the three-quarter line opposite (see page 59), which is not a marked line, but something you will have to judge. 10m circles are smaller again, but you will get quite a lot of practice riding these figures, because, as mentioned, the turn down the centre line is ridden as a 10m half-circle and most turns through corners, or across the centre, are ridden more or less as quarters of a 10m circle.

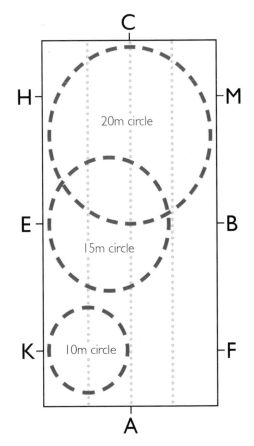

Examples of 10, 15 and 20m circles.

Performing a 20m circle.

A 5m loop. This is ridden by starting down a long side of the arena then, from a quarter marker, looping gradually off the outside track to reach the quarter line halfway up the arena, then looping back to regain the outside track at the further quarter marker. For example, on the right rein, you might ride from A, through the corner to K and, at K, begin a loop that is 5m in from the outside track (i.e. touching the quarter line) level with E. From there, you complete the loop to rejoin the outside track at H.

Performing a 5m loop.

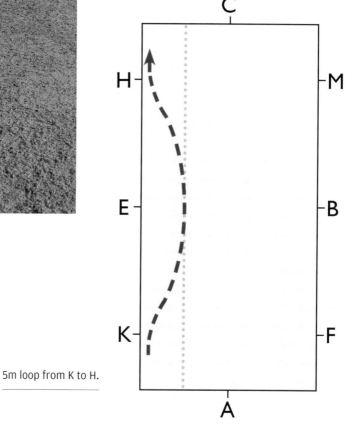

5m loop from K to H.

Serpentine. In simple terms, a series of big, evenly sized loops, each of which changes direction from the previous loop. The most basic serpentine, beginning at A or C in a 20 × 40m arena, is the two-loop figure made up of two 20m half-circles (for example, from C on the right rein, a 20m half-circle to X, followed immediately by a 20m half-circle left to A. In the 20m × 60m arena, a similar serpentine made up with 20m half-circles would have three loops, the middle one of which would pass either side of the X marker. See serpentine diagrams overleaf.

below Three-loop serpentine stage one.

lower photo Three-loop serpentine stage two.

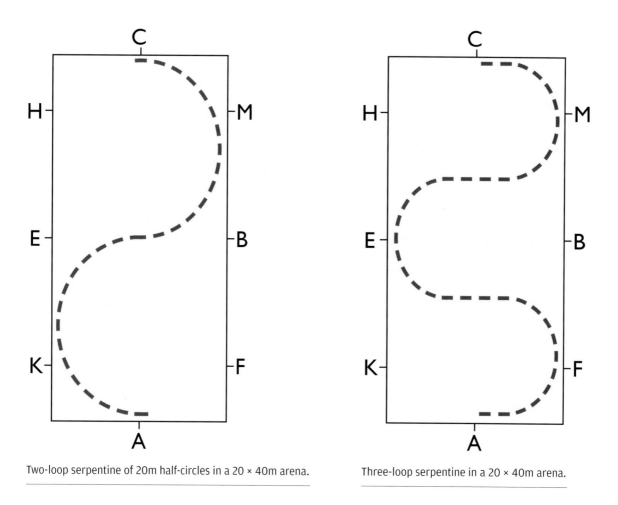

Two-loop serpentine of 20m half-circles in a 20 × 40m arena.

Three-loop serpentine in a 20 × 40m arena.

- Serpentines with an even number of loops can be used to change the rein; those with an odd number of loops end up on the same rein as they started on.

- Serpentines with loops smaller than 20m are ridden as half-circles connected by straight lines.

- All serpentines require a smooth change of flexion, bend and diagonal over the centre line. The more loops in a serpentine, and thus the smaller each loop, the harder it is to ride accurately.

Arena etiquette

When riding in the arena with others, there are certain rules that you must adhere to so that you don't crash into one another.

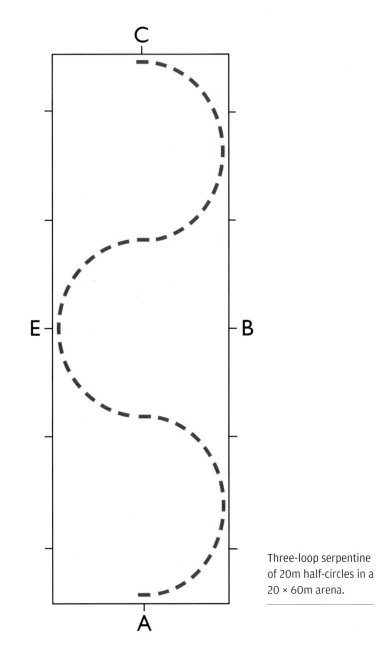

Three-loop serpentine of 20m half-circles in a 20 × 60m arena.

- Make sure you are aware of where the other riders are going so you do not ride into them.

- When riding behind another horse, allow at least one and a half horse's lengths between you and the horse in front so you and your horse do not get kicked, and you also have time to stop or turn away if the one in front stops suddenly.

- Turn across the school if you need to overtake a slower rider, making sure you give them plenty of room if you are getting too close to them.

- If a horse is going in the opposite direction to you (on the other rein), always pass left shoulder to left shoulder.

- Walk only on the inner track, to allow others to trot and canter on the outside track without being impeded.

- Unless you are halting briefly between periods of walk, it is best to halt across the centre of the school, where you are least likely to impede other riders.

- Do not use your whip when you are next to another horse as this may upset him and cause that rider to lose control of their horse.

CHAPTER SEVEN

YOUR FIRST RIDING LESSON

During your first lesson it is totally normal for you to be either on a lead rein or have an instructor walking right next to the horse to help you control him. Normally you will start on a one-to-one basis as this means it is easier for the instructor to teach you basic control and be able to help you if you are struggling. There is no specific number of private lessons you need before riding becomes easier, as everyone learns at different speeds. It will depend on your own personal confidence level, how easy you find it to balance on the horse and how easy you find it to be in control. Your instructor should be able to judge how well you are doing and whether you are ready to join a group lesson. Once basic stopping, starting and steering have been mastered and you are able to walk and trot safely, the next step is joining in a group lesson.

A group lesson can have a varied number of riders but normally between three and eight. It can be more fun to ride in a group and it is a good way to make new friends at the riding centre. Remember you can always have a one-to-one with your instructor if you feel a little out of your depth or need a little extra help.

Bear in mind that, while it is great fun, riding like all sports, does require a lot of practice to become proficient – so don't worry if you find it a bit daunting at first. The main object is to enjoy it and work with the horse.

A group lesson involves a number of other riders joining you.

Mounting

This chapter deals with the principles of mounting and dismounting and the rider's basic position in the saddle. As mentioned above, it is likely nowadays that your first lesson will be one-to-one and it is almost certain that you will first be taught how to get on from a mounting block. However, it is possible, at some stage, that you will need to mount from the ground in company (whether as part of a group lesson or not). If this is the case then, as described later under Dismounting, it's important not to allow horses to get too close to each other. They like their own space and horses who are standing too close may kick out or bite each other. Trying to mount in a confined space amongst fidgety horses is both difficult and dangerous.

The reins

Once you are ready to mount, the first thing you will need to do is to put the reins over the horse's head back to their correct position. While you are standing by the horse's shoulder, and facing forwards to his head, look at the reins and divide them in your hands so that the left one is in the left and the right one in your right. Hold them about three-quarters of the way down near to the central buckle and hold your hands apart. Now you should have a loop and this can be carefully passed up and over the horse's ears and behind his head. The reins can then be pulled down his neck and slightly to the left side.

TOP TIPS >
HOLDING THE REINS WHEN ADJUSTING TACK

There will be times when you need to adjust your tack, such as tightening your girth or changing the length of your stirrup leathers while holding your horse. To do this, put your arm through the reins and let them rest in the crook of your elbow as you check your tack. This means the reins are not dangling on the ground and you still have control of the horse while using both hands for the next task.

below Passing the reins over the horse's head.

1 Make a loop with the horse's reins.

2 Gently pass them over the horse's ears.

3 Place them at the base of the horse's neck by his withers.

Checking the girth from the ground

Now you will need to check your girth to ensure it is holding the saddle in place tightly enough for you to get on. To check the girth, place your hand between the girth and horse's side to see how slack it is. If you can get more than two fingers' width between the horse's side and the girth, then you will need to tighten it before you can mount, otherwise the saddle will slip round when you put your foot in the stirrup.

To tighten the girth, use one hand to lift the saddle flap above your shoulder and let it rest there. Over the girth buckles is the buckle guard, a small flap of leather, which can either be lifted or pulled up out of the way to expose the girth straps and girth buckles. Normally there are three straps and the girth is fastened to the first and second strap or the first and third strap for safety and the horse's comfort. One hand can now move down and pull the girth strap up, while the other hand is used to put the tongue of the buckle into the hole in the girth strap. Be careful not to let the material of your glove become snagged in the tongue of the buckle.

Repeat this with the other strap so they are both of an equal length. Ideally the girth needs to be evenly secured symmetrically on each side of the saddle to create the most even pressure for a comfortable fit – i.e. not on the bottom holes on one side of the saddle and the top on the other. Once you have tightened the girth, re-check it and then pull the buckle guard back down so it covers the girth buckles and protects the saddle

below Checking and tightening a girth.

1 Check the tightness of the girth by placing your fingers behind it.

2 Lift the saddle flap and the girth guard.

3 Tighten the girth and lower the saddle flap.

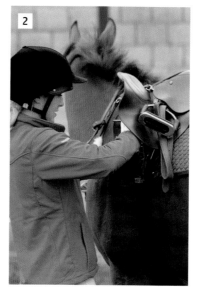

flap. Ideally you should just be able to slide two fingers between the girth and the horse's side.

The girth will need to be re-checked once you are on board and possibly again once you have walked around on the horse for a few minutes. This is because horses can sometimes 'blow out' their ribs making it harder for you to do the girth up. Once the horse relaxes, the girth can feel loose again and will need tightening before working him further. When doing up the girth, watch out for the horse being grumpy as not all horses enjoy having their girths tightened. A horse may have had a bad experience where his girth was wrenched up too tight, or the girth pinched his skin, and it can make him wary of having his girth done up. Watch out for him bringing his head round and trying to nip you. Use the reins to keep his head straight or get someone to help you by holding the horse for you.

Checking the stirrups from the ground

When the horse is tacked up, the stirrups are not left dangling down, but are 'run up' to the tops of the stirrup leathers so they are out of the

way when the horse is being tacked up, led about, or when the saddle is being stored. The stirrup leather is a long strap held in a loop by a buckle and the stirrup iron hangs off it. The buckle sits up under the skirt of the saddle and hangs from the stirrup bar. The spare end of the stirrup leather either slots through a small loop of leather behind where the rider's leg sits, or fits through a slot in the saddle flap to keep it out of the rider's way.

To 'run the stirrup down', stand facing the saddle and lift the leather loop out from the iron. Then, with the hand nearest to the horse's head, hold the pommel (front) area of the saddle. The other hand can now take hold of the stirrup iron and pull it straight down the stirrup leather to the end. Both stirrups will need to be run down before you can get on.

It's important that your stirrups are adjusted to the correct length for the length of your legs and the easiest way to check this is to make a fist with your hand, place it at the top of the leather by the stirrup bar and pull the iron down your arm into your armpit. Ideally the stirrup length will be from your fist to your armpit, which is similar to

A stirrup run up.

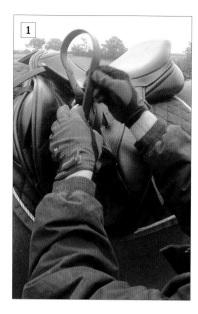

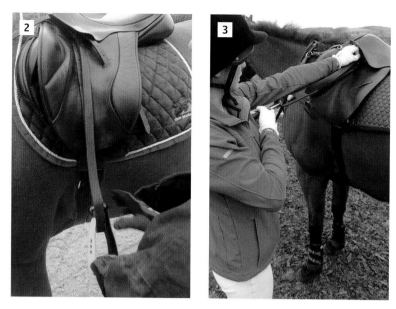

Adjusting stirrups from the ground.

1 Take the stirrup leather out of the stirrup iron.

2 Pull the iron down the leather.

3 To check the length, hold the iron under your armpit and place your balled-fist up by the skirt of the saddle.

the inside of your thigh to the floor. This method usually gives a working approximation of length, but minor adjustments may still be necessary once you are mounted – initially subject to your instructor's advice.

TOP TIPS › EQUAL LENGTH

The stirrup leathers need to be equal in length to help distribute the rider's weight evenly over the horse's back. If, despite having both leathers adjusted to the same numbered hole, one always feels shorter than the other, consider your own posture and whether any previous injury has made one leg shorter than another, or caused you to put more weight into one stirrup. If you are aware of such an injury, you should tell your instructor, who can take it into account and perhaps offer some advice. Additionally, a trained physiotherapist should be able to give you some exercises to help even up your posture.

Mounting from a mounting block

When it is time to mount, your instructor will ask you to lead your horse to the mounting block to help you get on. The mounting block can be a wooden block or a purpose-built raised area. Steps or a ramp enable you to climb onto the top of the block so you are above ground level. It is traditional to mount from the left side of the horse so the horse will need to be positioned on the right-hand side of the block as this will allow you to mount from his left side, which will be closest to the block. Ideally, the horse needs to be close to but not touching the block, with his saddle next to the highest part so you can easily reach the left stirrup. The best way to get the horse straight and parallel to the block is to walk him towards it on a straight line – turning him tightly towards it will make it difficult to line him up. Normally your instructor will also help by leading the horse from the other side and help keep him parallel to the block.

The horse is held still with his saddle adjacent to the part of the block you are standing on. When you are learning, it is easier to lead the horse to the block with your instructor and then, whilst the instructor holds the horse, you can climb up onto the block. Once you progress, you will be able to lead the horse to the block and climb up onto it at the same time.

The instructor will hold the stirrup on their side of the horse (the right) to counteract your weight and help stabilise the saddle, preventing it from slipping over to your side.

Next, take both reins in your left hand and hold them by the horse's neck in front of the saddle. The left hand will now also need to hold both the reins and the pommel of the saddle. With your right hand, take hold of the stirrup iron and turn the outside edge slightly towards you in an anticlockwise direction and place your left foot into it, making sure the ball of your foot is across the stirrup tread. Your right hand can now be placed over to the right-hand side of the saddle on the skirt (which covers the stirrup buckle).

Bend your right leg slightly then, keeping pressure in the left stirrup, use your right leg to spring and push yourself up off the mounting block. Your right leg then swings over the saddle and horse's back and, as it does so, you will need to bend slightly at the waist and keep your bodyweight low over the horse's withers. Once your right leg is clearly over the horse and you have landed gently on the horse's back, you can sit up centrally in the saddle and place your right foot in the stirrup iron. Once both feet are in the irons, sit straight in the saddle and hold the reins – one in each hand.

Mounting from a block.

1 Stand on the mounting block, hold your reins in your left hand by the withers and place your left foot in the stirrup iron.

2 Push off against the mounting block and pass your right leg over the horse's back without touching him.

3 Sit gently in the saddle and place your right foot in the stirrup iron.

TOP TIPS > MOUNTING CLEANLY

As you are mounting, try not to poke the horse in the side with your toe, or kick his hindquarters as you take your leg over him. Try to land lightly in the saddle and ensure your whip (see next chapter) is in your left hand when mounting.

A mounting block not only makes it easier for you to get onto the horse, but it is also kinder to the horse's back as it prevents the saddle from being yanked over to one side and putting pressure on the horse's spine when the rider mounts from the ground. There can be a considerable sideways pull on the saddle when you mount from the ground, which, over time, can strain the horse's back. Once you are able to mount the horse easily then you can do so without the instructor helping you.

Mounting from the ground

As just mentioned, it is also possible to mount from the ground, although you will need to be fairly agile and able to spring up off the ground as you mount to make it easier. Normally, mounting from the ground is only used in a situation where there is no available mounting block, such as out on a ride in the countryside. To mount from the ground, it is better to have a helper as they can hold the stirrup on the right-hand side of the horse to prevent the saddle being pulled across the horse's back. One of their hands will hold the horse still while the other holds the stirrup iron.

With your left hand, hold the reins and pommel of the saddle while you stand by the horse's shoulder area and face your body slightly towards the horse's hindquarters. With your right hand, turn the stirrup iron anti-clockwise about 5cm (2in) so you can place the ball of your left foot onto the stirrup tread. Then place your right hand onto the top of the saddle near the front on the opposite side. Bounce up and down on your right leg and hop closer to the horse while turning to face slightly towards the front of the horse. (If the horse is on the big side for you, it can be helpful to let the stirrup leather down a few holes to facilitate mounting from the ground – but don't overdo this or you may struggle to get your right leg over the horse's back.) Now push up from your right leg and increase the pressure in your left foot as the right foot leaves the ground. You need to make sure you spring upwards with enough power to enable your right leg to clear the back of the saddle and the horse's quarters – just like you did during mounting from the block. When you land on the saddle make sure that you take a little pressure on your arms to balance and take some of the weight on landing. That way, you don't land heavily on the horse's back, which would be uncomfortable for him. See photos overleaf.

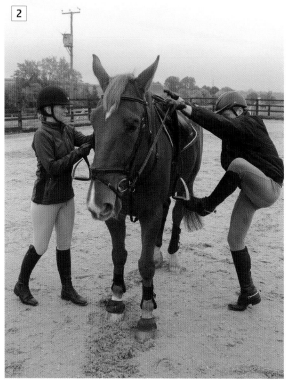

this page and opposite Mounting from the ground.

1 Place the reins in the left hand and hold them up by the horse's withers, and balance on your right leg.

2 Place your left foot in the stirrup iron.

3 Bend your right knee.

4 Push off with your right leg and put more weight into the left stirrup to push yourself up.

5 Carefully pass your right leg over the horse's hindquarters.

6 Sit gently in the saddle and sit up.

7 Place your feet in the stirrup irons.

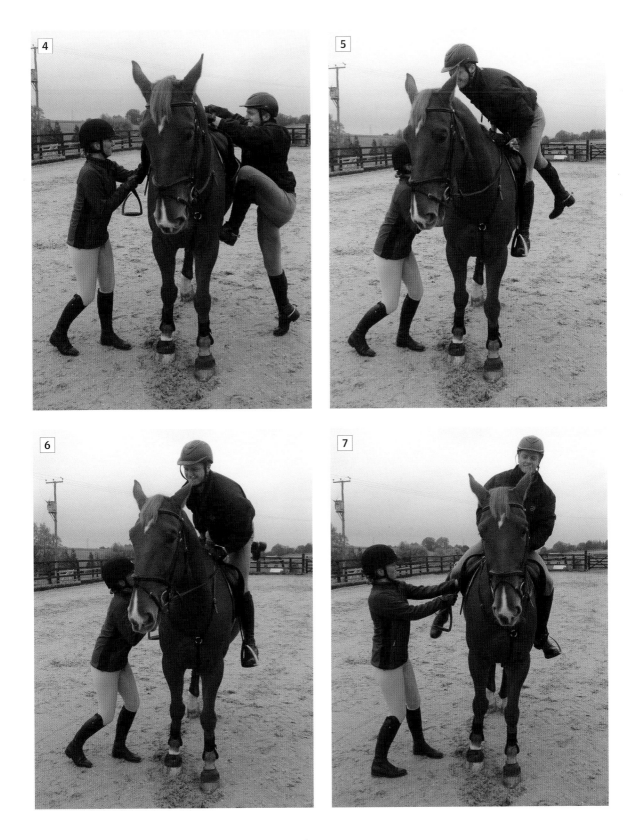

Mounting with a leg-up

Another way of mounting is by getting a leg-up. This may be used when there is no mounting block and the horse is too tall for you to mount successfully from the ground. A capable helper is needed for this to work effectively.

Their job is to help push you upwards when you spring up to the horse's back. First, stand next to the horse's girth and face the saddle. Lift your left leg and bend it to 90 degrees at the knee. Your helper then uses both hands to hold your leg on the shin area. They need to stand to the left of you and face slightly towards the back of the horse. As you bounce up and down on your right leg, on the count of three, you spring up as they also push you up, holding your bent leg (which you must keep in this position otherwise, as they push, your leg will fold and it won't work). It is very important that they bend their knees before pushing you so they push and stand up to create maximum power to help get you into the air.

Once you are astride, place your feet in the stirrups, sit up and shorten your reins.

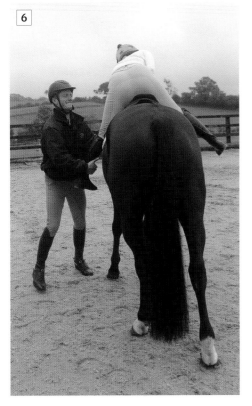

opposite page and here Mounting with a leg-up.

1 Ask a helper to take hold of your bent left leg with two hands.

2 Count to three while bouncing and, on bounce three, push against the helper's hands on your leg.

3 Make sure you spring upwards to get enough height.

4 Pass your right leg carefully over the horse's hindquarters without kicking him.

5 Take the weight onto your arms and against the helper's hands.

6 Land gently in the saddle.

7 Place your feet in the stirrups.

Taking hold of the reins

The reins are held through your palms, with the little finger on the outside and the thumb over the top. Hold the buckle of the reins in one hand and slightly up off the horse's neck. Keep your other hand with the thumb uppermost and fingers forwards – as if you are going to shake someone's hand. Place the rein across your palm. Now close all your fingers around the rein. Next, place your thumb on the top like a little roof. Finally take your little finger out and around the rein so the rein is now lying between that finger and your ring finger. Repeat with your other hand and then make sure your hands are either side of the horse's neck and level – as though you were holding a tray.

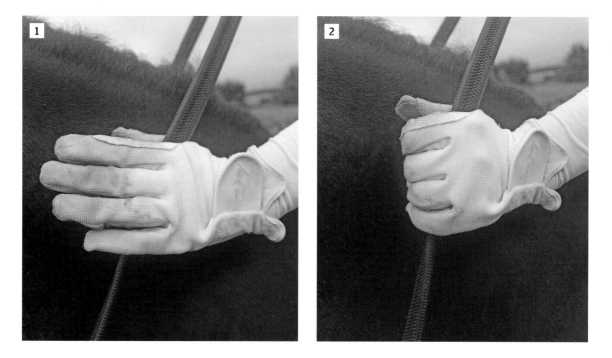

above and opposite page Holding the reins.

1 Place the rein in your left hand lying flat across your palm.

2 Close your hand around the rein.

3 Hook your little finger under the rein.

4 Place your thumb on top of the rein.

5 An inside view of the rein in the rider's hand.

6 How to hold the reins viewed from above.

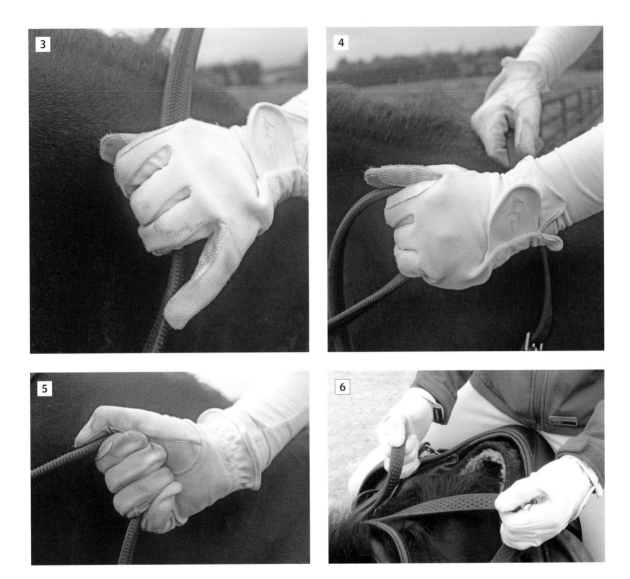

TOP TIPS › HOW TIGHT?

Hold your hand round the rein as though you were holding an egg. An open hand will let it go but a tight hand will crush it! The hands needs to be flexible so you can adapt to the movement of the horse and be able to follow the contact created by the reins between you and the horse's mouth. The horse's mouth is very sensitive and you don't want to harm or upset him by being rough.

Shortening the reins

The reins can be shortened by using a sliding movement down the leather. Start by holding the correct rein in each hand. With the left hand, take hold of the right rein, using your thumb so that you still have hold of both reins. Then slide your right hand down the rein and close the fingers around the rein before bringing that hand back towards you and so making the rein shorter. Repeat with the other hand to make the reins equal in length.

Checks and adjustments while mounted

Checking the girth while mounted

The girth can be checked on either side of the horse. When you are mounted, put both the reins into one hand and let your other hand hang down in front of you. Then bend forwards and slightly over the shoulder of the horse and slide your free hand under the girth from the front. If you can fit more than two fingers under it, then it will need to be tightened. To do this, sit back up in the saddle but keep both the reins in one hand. Keep your feet in the stirrups and then lift the leg on the side of your free hand (the side on which you wish to adjust the girth) forwards and upwards so it rests on the saddle above the knee roll, with your foot pointing towards the direction of the horse's head. Use your free hand and lift the saddle flap up on that side. You should be able to move the buckle guard upwards to expose the girth buckles. Use your hand to pull the strap upwards and your first finger to push the tongue of the buckle into the next hole up on the girth strap. Repeat on the other strap then pull the girth guard back down, lower the saddle flap and lower your leg back down. If necessary, swap your reins over and use your freed hand to repeat the adjustment on the other side of the saddle if the girth needs to be done up evenly on each side.

Adjusting the stirrups while mounted

It is much safer to adjust your stirrup leathers with your feet still in the irons, but it does take a bit of practice. Put the reins into one hand (the hand on the other side from where you want to adjust the leather) and keep your free hand near the pommel of the saddle. Then, with the stirrup leather

Checking and adjusting the girth from the saddle.

1 Place the reins in one hand and move your leg up and in front of the saddle.

2 Lift the saddle flap.

3 Use your finger to pull the strap up.

4 Place the tongue in the hole.

5 Re-check the tightness of the girth by placing your fingers between the girth and your horse's side. If necessary, you can now swap the reins from one hand to the other and repeat on the other side.

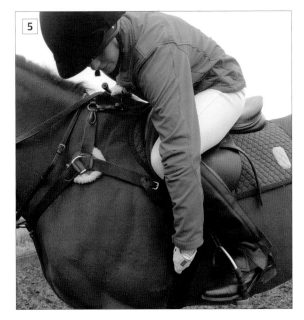

you are going to adjust, turn your thigh and knee away and outwards from the saddle. Keep the ball of your foot in the stirrup iron but slightly release any downward pressure on that iron. You should now be able to place your free hand in front of your thigh and pull the end of the leather out from its keeper. Now grasp the buckle from under the skirt and pull it a few centimetres away from the stirrup bar. You will now be able to adjust the buckle to a higher hole to raise the stirrup or a lower hole to lower the stirrup. Once the length has been changed, you will need to feed the underside of the leather back under the stirrup bar so that the buckle can lie back under the skirt. Pull up on the uppermost part of the leather to lift the leather up through the slot on the stirrup iron and, while keeping it in position, use a little pressure on your foot in the stirrup iron to pull the underside down so the leather is pulled back through the stirrup bar in a see-saw motion. The spare end can then be re-threaded through the keeper. There is definitely a knack to this task but with practice it will become easier.

Check the adjustment of your stirrups by seeing if you can easily stand up and balance in them by maintaining a slight bend in your legs. If they are too long, standing and balancing will be very difficult. If they are too short, your knees will probably be over the knee rolls of the saddle when you are sitting in the saddle and, when you stand, you will be a little too high above the saddle and will feel unbalanced.

right and opposite page
Checking and adjusting the length of stirrup leathers from the saddle.

1 Put the reins into one hand and turn your foot and knee away from the saddle.

2 Using your spare hand, pull the stirrup buckle up and away from under the saddle skirt and adjust the buckle.

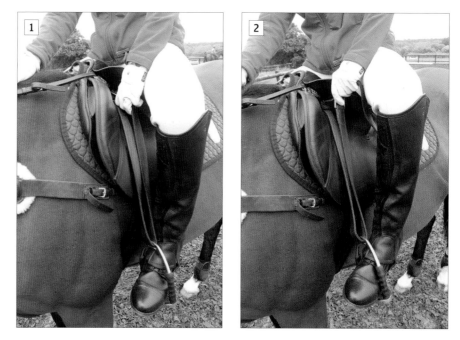

3 Pull the stirrup leather down so that the buckle sits back up under the skirt.

4 Get your instructor to stand in front of you and check that your stirrups are level.

Rider's position in halt

How do I stay on? Standing in the stirrups even in halt can be a challenge for someone who has never ridden before. It's important not to grip with your legs if you feel unsteady in the saddle, because the horse has been taught that squeezing with the legs means go forwards and he may confuse your squeezing with asking him to go faster. In fact a correct position, with weight down into the saddle, and down 'through' the legs, with the assistance of gravity, actually increases stability.

If you look at the photo of the rider taken from the side in halt, there should be an imaginary vertical line drawn from the ear down through the shoulder, hip and heel.

The head should be held up and central, with the neck gently pressing against the collar of the shirt.

right There should be an imaginary line from the rider's ear, shoulder, hip and heel.

right The head should sit centrally above the shoulders which are parallel to the ground.

far right The feet should be parallel to the ground, and level.

The rider should be able to sit tall and straight in their upper body and have both shoulders level.

The arms are relaxed and the upper arms lie straight down by the sides of the body, but with a bend at the elbows. The forearms are held in front of the body, the hands being held upright but gently closed (as though carrying a mug of water), with the thumbs resting uppermost on top of the hands.

Both legs need to hang relaxed and at an equal length with a gentle bend at the knee. The balls of the feet rest across the stirrup treads with the heels a fraction lower than the toes. The ankles flex naturally and the whole of the leg has a slight 'Z' shape which enables the rider to sit and rise in trot or rise easily in the saddle when jumping or galloping as the 'Z' shape (the flexion of the joints) acts as a shock-absorber.

Looking at a rider from behind, the head should sit centrally above the shoulders, which are level and parallel to the ground. The torso is equally balanced on both sides, with the spine in a straight line. The legs hang naturally and evenly in length. The feet need to be parallel to the horse's sides so the toes do not stick out as this will cause the legs to be stiff and gripping.

Common positional faults

1. Lower leg too far forwards.

2. Lower leg too far back.

3. Rider leaning back.

4. Rider's body tipping/curling forwards.

5. From the back, sitting unevenly, with collapsed upper body and one leg longer.

Dismounting

The correct term for getting off the horse is dismounting. First, you will need to halt the horse on the centre line of the arena facing towards the long side. If you are in a group lesson with several riders (which may not be the case initially, but will in due course), then make sure you leave at least 2m between your horse and the ones either side of him. Each horse likes their own personal space and this will also give you enough room to get off and move either side of your horse without being in the kicking zone of another horse.

When you are sure that the horse is standing still under your control (for how to halt, see Chapter 9), hold both reins and whip in your left hand. The left hand needs to remain close to the saddle or withers as it can rest there to help balance you during dismounting. Your right hand can now be placed onto the right skirt of the saddle. This right arm is going to help support you when you swing your leg over the saddle. Take both feet out of the stirrups.

Now, in one movement, bend forwards at your waist and use your right arm to stabilise your body while you swing your right leg backwards and up over the horse's back. Keep your right leg straight so it doesn't get caught on the cantle as you swing it over the saddle. Both legs will now be on the left side of the horse and you can slide down his side, landing on both feet and bending your knees to help absorb the impact before

opposite page and here How to dismount.

1 First, take both your feet out of the stirrups.

2 Then lean your shoulders forward over the horse's withers.

3 Pass the right leg over the horse's hindquarters.

4 Make sure you don't kick him with your leg.

5 Take both legs over the side of the horse.

6 Land and bend your knees.

7 Stand up straight.

standing up straight. Your left hand still has hold of the reins so you remain in control of the horse.

Now you can take the reins over the horse's head, run up both stirrups and loosen the girth before standing back on the left-hand side of the horse, holding him with one hand on the reins at the bit and the loop of the reins in the other hand.

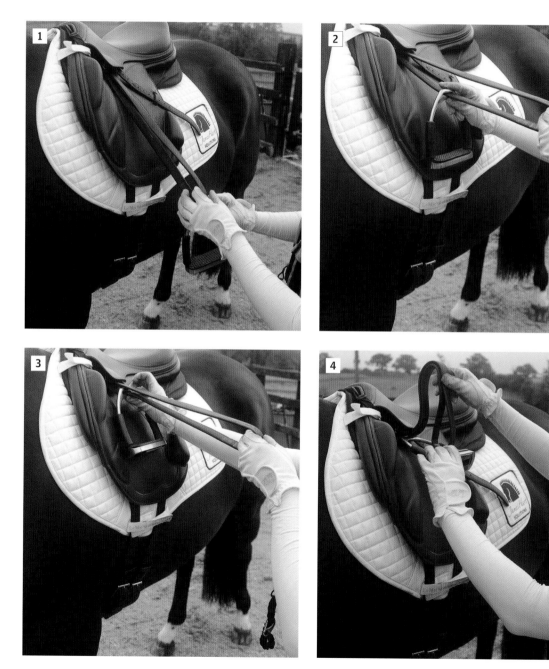

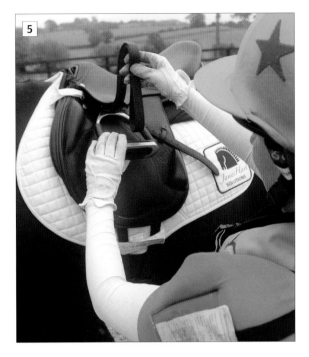

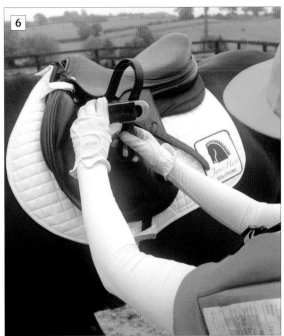

opposite and above

How to run up the stirrups.

1 To run up the stirrup, take the stirrup iron in your left hand.

2 Pass the iron up the lower piece of the stirrup leather.

3 Pass it all the way to the top.

4 Gather up the stirrup leather.

5 Pass it through the stirrup iron.

6 Pull it all the way through.

CHAPTER **EIGHT**

MOVING OFF – UNDERSTANDING THE AIDS

The natural aids

The rider's natural aids are the voice, weight, seat, legs and hands and these aids are used to help control the horse. They are used to ask the horse to stop, move, change direction and a skilled rider can use them to help balance the horse and improve his movement during training.

The voice

The voice can be used firmly to get the horse to react and move forwards, such as 'walk on'. A clicking sound can also be made to encourage the horse forwards as it is a sharp sound. The voice can also be used in a soothing way to ask the horse to steady or calm down. The word 'whoa' is commonly used around horses because, when it is said in a gentle and soothing manner, the horse has been trained to understand it as a slowing command.

Weight and seat

The rider's weight can be used to direct the horse and also to help adjust his gait and speed. When you are sitting astride the horse, your bodyweight needs to be positioned centrally in the saddle. If you are not sitting

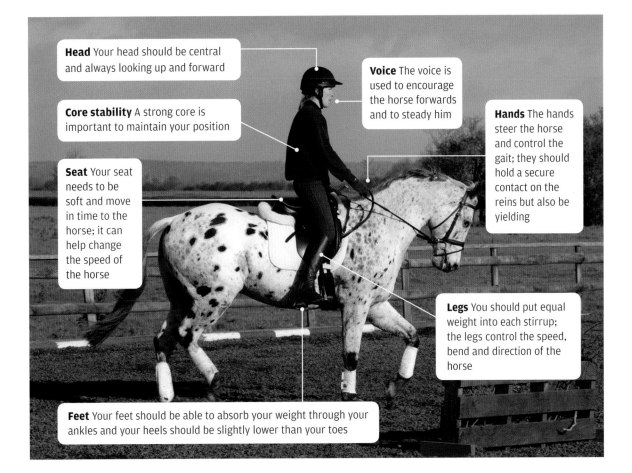

Head Your head should be central and always looking up and forward

Voice The voice is used to encourage the horse forwards and to steady him

Core stability A strong core is important to maintain your position

Hands The hands steer the horse and control the gait; they should hold a secure contact on the reins but also be yielding

Seat Your seat needs to be soft and move in time to the horse; it can help change the speed of the horse

Legs You should put equal weight into each stirrup; the legs control the speed, bend and direction of the horse

Feet Your feet should be able to absorb your weight through your ankles and your heels should be slightly lower than your toes

Parts of the rider's body and what they do.

in balance, then the horse will also not be in balance and as the speed of the gait increases, the effect becomes more pronounced.

In order to be in harmony with the movement and direction of the horse, you need to mirror the horse's movement without collapsing your body position, with a slight shift of your weight to the direction of travel. When travelling in a straight line, your upper body needs to remain tall and upright unless doing rising trot, when you incline your shoulders slightly forwards. (When you progress to light-seat canter, galloping, and jumping, you will incline your upper body forward as appropriate, but these things come later in the learning process.) When turning or going round a corner, your upper body will need to turn and stay in line with the horse's shoulders as they turn. By turning through your ribcage, your weight will also mirror the direction of the horse.

When thinking about your weight, also remember your seat. Don't let your weight get left behind the motion of the horse, or off to one side.

top When riding a circle or corner, your upper body needs to remain tall.

above Your upper body should turn and stay in line with the horse's shoulders.

right Turn through your ribcage.

MOVING OFF – UNDERSTANDING THE AIDS **99**

Your seat can be used to change the feeling on the horse's back, too. Normally when you are riding, your seat and bottom move gently in time with the motion of the horse's movement. However, your seat can be made heavier and kept stiller and this will help slow the horse down. It can also be made lighter to encourage the horse to move more freely forwards. The best way to achieve these effects is to think of your tummy as a round balloon. To increase the pressure down onto your seat bones, push your tummy down to make the balloon an oval shape. To lighten, breathe up into your ribcage. These adjustments are small and take practice but can be included to refine your riding technique.

The legs

Legs are very important aids in riding. They control speed, bend in the horse's body and direction of movement. Once the leg aid has been applied, the legs should then be allowed to hang close to the horse's sides without a continued pressure. Continual use of the legs every stride either results in the horse becoming bored and ignoring your leg aids, or becoming faster and faster. Try to use your legs like a switch; only use them when necessary rather than continually nagging at the horse.

Applying both legs together just level to the girth will ask for forward motion. Applying one leg near the girth with a small amount of pressure and one leg slightly behind the girth with a small pressure will encourage the horse to bend, such as when riding on a circle.

One leg back with more pressure will ask the horse to move away from that pressure and so make a sideways movement with his hindquarters. This can be controlled by the other leg also pushing the horse forwards to move sideways on a shallow angle, or by the reins feeling the horse's mouth and slowing him down so he moves sideways on a steeper angle. However, the aid for canter is inside leg by the girth and outside leg about 10cm (some instructors use the term 'a hand span') behind the girth. In this case, both legs squeeze gently at the same time to make it clear to him that it is not a sideways aid.

When moving one leg back, this should be done from the hip, not the knee. In this way the basic leg position is maintained, with the heel lower than the toe.

The rider's leg resting on the girth. From here, it can be applied with various degrees of pressure to ask for forward movement.

The rider's leg back behind the girth.

The hands

Your hands communicate down the reins to the bit, which sits in the horse's mouth. The mouth is fairly sensitive and so your hands need to develop an elastic feel on the reins to give the horse a pleasant contact. When people are learning to ride, there is a tendency to use the reins to help balance, which is not pleasant for the horse. Also, it is important that the hands do not make involuntary movements, particularly up and down, but a rider cannot completely avoid these movements by thinking solely of the hands – a stable overall posture is required for this. Therefore, it is important to develop your own balance, both so that it is independent of the reins, and so that minor deficiencies don't cause unwarranted changes in the rein contact. Lunge lessons (see Chapter 11) can be very helpful in this respect.

The hands normally have a very gentle feel on the reins. This creates a 'contact' to the mouth. The hands can be used together with an increased pressure as a non-allowing ('holding') aid to ask the horse to slow down or stop. When asking the horse to slow with the reins, you must also support the horse with your legs (by having them gently on his sides, without gripping) as this helps him position his own legs underneath his body and to be more balanced in a downward transition.

When turning the horse with the aids, both leg and rein aids need to be used. As an example, to ask the horse to turn to the left, the rider needs to slightly open the inside* (left) rein away from the left side of the horse's neck (i.e. the hand moves out, not back) with a little pressure in the direction of the turn. This asks the horse to bend his neck towards the direction of the turn. The outside (right) rein is yielded slightly to allow the bend that has been produced in the horse's neck. These aids both invite and allow the horse to turn left. (To turn right, the same principles are applied, but the right rein will be the inside rein, and the left rein the outside one.)

The tightness of the turn is controlled by the amount of pressure on the inside rein – although this pressure should not be too strong or it will bend the horse's neck too much and then he will lose balance, and his ability to move smoothly through the turn will be impeded. In fact, any over-strong uses of the rein aids are likely to have such effects, and will make the horse uncomfortable and unsteady in his head-carriage and reluctant to move forwards, which is why stiff elbows, forearms and wrists are to be avoided. It will help you to give subtle rein aids (through an elastic and springy feel on the reins) if you think about changing the contact with your fingers

*Note 'Inside' refers to the inside of any bend in the horse's body. For riding exercises at novice level (and often beyond) this will nearly always be the inside of the arena, too, but in some advanced work, this may not be the case.

rather than making bigger movements with your arms. Thus the contact can be increased by closing your fingers more around the rein, and it can be reduced by opening the fingers slightly (remember the idea of holding an egg in your hands in Top Tips page 35).

In addition to allowing the horse to move into a turn, the outside rein is needed to help ride out of the turn. As you complete the turn, you need to relax the feel on the inside rein and add a little pressure on the outside rein to help straighten the horse's neck. Once the turn has been completed, both reins need to have an equal contact to keep the horse straight and allow him to move forwards in the new direction.

The turning aids just described are based upon what is called an open rein aid (the inside rein is opened, as explained). Once you have good control of your body, and can apply the aids subtly, in correct combination, your instructor may introduce you to other rein aids, which have different effects for more advanced purposes.

Artificial aids: whip and spurs

The whip

The whip is a secondary aid to the leg, rather than an instrument of punishment. It is held in your inside hand with the handle through your palm and the fingers closed around the handle. The shaft of the whip then lies diagonally across your thigh so the flap or lash end is pointing towards the horse's hindquarters behind your leg. The whip can be used on the flank, quarters and shoulder of the horse as an aid to encourage him forwards, to ask for more power when exercising him, or to help with keeping him straight during exercise.

Holding the reins and whip correctly.

Whips can be either short (75cm) or long (usually 110cm) and are nowadays made from a synthetic material. The end that fits in your hand has a handle that is thicker. The rest of the whip then tapers down to a loop of leather or thin lash. A long whip can be used to flick the horse gently behind your leg on his flank, without the need to take your hand off the reins. When using a short whip, you will need to put the reins into the hand that is not holding the whip and use the whip on the horse's side behind your leg.

Changing the whip over

As mentioned, the whip is normally carried in your inside hand when riding in the arena. However, it can be carried in either hand and will need to be changed from one hand to the other when you change direction ('change the rein') during your lesson.

Most trained horses are used to a rider carrying a whip; however, to change a whip efficiently and without waving it about and scaring the horse does take some practice.

To change a short whip over, the reins are put into the hand that is also holding the whip. The other hand then begins to pull the whip upwards and out through that hand. The whip is now in the other hand and can be taken over the horse's neck and that hand can now re-take the appropriate rein.

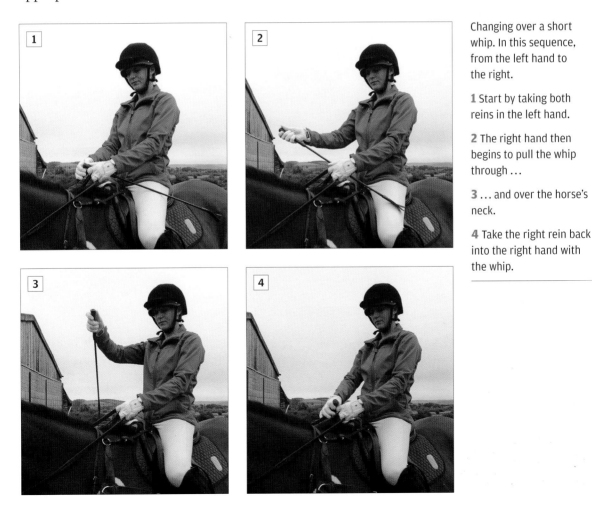

Changing over a short whip. In this sequence, from the left hand to the right.

1 Start by taking both reins in the left hand.

2 The right hand then begins to pull the whip through …

3 … and over the horse's neck.

4 Take the right rein back into the right hand with the whip.

Changing over a long whip.

1 Start by taking the reins into the hand which is holding the whip.

2 With the other hand, reach over and take the handle of the long whip with your fingers facing your body.

3 Turn your hand over so that the end of the whip performs a semi-circle in the air over the horse's withers.

4 Bring the whip all the way over until it is lying on the other side of the horse by his shoulder.

5 Place the whip over your thigh and take the rein back into the left hand along with the whip.

To change a long whip over, both reins are placed into the hand that is holding the whip. This leaves one hand free and this can now reach over the top of the other hand. Take hold of the whip at the lower end of the handle and, as you turn your hand over and towards the correct side of the horse's neck, the flap or lash end will perform a semi-circle in the air above the horse. When you are practised at this method, you will be able to change the whip over without having to let go of the reins. To do this, the hand with the whip turns over in the direction of your thumb. The lash end then rises up above the horse's neck and the other hand will be able to take the handle and finish bringing the whip down towards the new side. This way, the reins stay in each hand and this is a safer way to change the whip when the horse is in motion. See the photo sequence opposite.

Spurs

You may see experienced riders wearing spurs and wonder what their actual use is. Rather than being used to goad or punish the horse, they are used discreetly to refine the leg aids and, to that purpose, are worn only by experienced riders who have complete control over the position and effectiveness of their leg aids.

Spurs are made of a band of metal with a shank at the back. They are attached by a leather strap that passes under the sole of the rider's boot, through slots on the band of metal on the side of the foot and then fastened over the top of the foot.

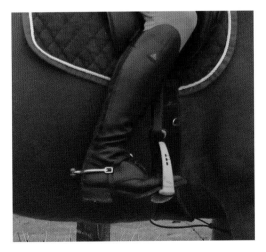

Experienced riders who have full control of their leg position may wear spurs, which are used to refine the leg aids.

CHAPTER NINE

HALT – WALK – TROT (RISING AND SITTING) AND STEERING

> **TOP TIPS > MINIMUM PRESSURE NECESSARY**
>
> Remember to use the minimum pressure with legs and hands necessary to achieve the desired effect. When the horse moves forward, the contact can be softened slightly so your arms are able to move with his movement.

Halt to walk

Make sure you have shortened your reins so you can feel the horse's mouth, but without pulling. Both legs can now squeeze at the same time on the girth area.

To ask the horse to move from halt to walk, the aids are simply a gentle nudge from your lower legs (from your calf to your heel). Using the legs too hard may confuse the horse and make him move faster than you expected, so start with a soft aid and if he does not respond you can gradually increase the pressure until he moves. Once he starts to move, your legs will then ideally stay still and be relaxed. If you keep nudging or start to grip your legs on, he could mistake this for the cue to move much faster and break into a trot or canter. However, you may need to remind your horse gently with your legs if he is going too slowly, the point being that the aids should be applied as necessary and not unthinkingly. Your seat should be allowed to swing gently in time with the motion of the walk.

As the horse's legs are lifted and placed on the ground, you will feel a gentle side-to-side rocking motion in time to the hind legs as they step under his body. The horse's head will also move up and down so you will need to make sure your arms have a bend at the elbow and are relaxed so they can follow the motion and not restrict the horse by pulling him in the mouth.

Walk to trot

Make sure the reins are not too long and that you can gently feel the horse's mouth, then apply both legs as you did when asking for walk, but with a little more pressure.

To ask the horse to trot, a gentle squeeze or nudge near the girth area with both heels at the same time should be enough for him to move out of walk and begin trotting. A very lazy horse may need a bit more encouragement such as a kick with your heels or a tap with a whip on his side. As mentioned earlier, you should never 'nag' the horse needlessly in any gait but, if you sense that he is getting idle, you should act promptly to re-establish the level of activity you require. Riding like this will encourage the horse to be much more responsive to your aids, because you are eliminating those that are meaningless. (If the horse is already walking or trotting, there's little point in keeping asking him to do it, but if you sense he's about to slow down or stop, you can give a meaningful aid that tells him 'Oi, keep going'.)

Rising trot

There are two ways to ride the trot – rising trot and sitting trot. Rising trot is the most comfortable way for most riders to move in time to the motion of the horse, but it takes a bit of practice to get the timing right as it involves rising a little out of the saddle and sitting down again in time to the trot rhythm. When the horse trots, his back rises and falls, making things feel quite bumpy, and it is easy to get out of rhythm with the movement until you have developed better timing and balance. If you do get out of rhythm, you will fall back into the saddle after the 'rising' phase and this is not pleasant for the horse's back.

To master the rising trot, you will need to rise when the outside fore-leg is off the ground and sit when the outside foreleg is on the ground. When you are learning, your instructor will normally help you rise and sit in time to the trot rhythm by saying 'up, down' at the right moments. By rising on the command 'up' and sitting on 'down' you will quickly get the rhythm.

To help your balance, your legs need to be used like springs. Think about your legs being a 'Z' shape. To rise up and out of the saddle, keep your feet in the stirrups and the soles parallel to the ground with your weight down into your heels. When you rise, aim to keep your feet in that same position and then push your body up out of the saddle by straightening your knees a little. Your bottom should rise off the saddle by just a few centimetres. Your body can fold a little at the waist so that your shoulders are just a fraction in front of your hips – a maximum of a couple of centimetres. This makes the movement easier as your centre of gravity is a little lower. Think of the motion of the rise as a forward motion towards the pommel of the saddle rather than a vertical skyward movement.

Don't stand up completely as there is not enough time in the gait for you to do this. If you are completely vertical, your knees will be locked straight and you will lose your balance and thump back down onto the horse's back. Try to let the horse's back help push you out of the saddle rather than forcing yourself upwards.

You will need to sit back gently on the saddle after rising. The motion between the two phases should be smooth and under control. To start with, your instructor will probably make you rise up and down in halt and even in walk so you can learn the balance and be able to control the height of your rising.

Changing your diagonal

When the horse is going around the arena in a clockwise direction, this is called being on the right rein as your right hand will be on the inside. When trotting in this direction, you will need to be rising and sitting in time to the outside foreleg. You can check this visually by glancing momentarily at the horse's outside shoulder (in this example, the left one): when it appears to be moving backwards, that foot is on the ground, and you should be sitting. When you change the rein and go anticlock-

top left The rider in the 'sit' position of rising trot.

top right The rider in the 'rise' position of rising trot.

centre left Two riders showing the two stances of rising trot.

centre right Rider out of balance in the trot.

left Rider tipping forwards in the trot.

wise onto the left rein, you will have to change and rise in time to the new outside foreleg, as this helps to balance the horse. This is called 'changing your diagonal'. The easiest way to do it is to sit for an extra beat in the trot rhythm so it'll be 'up, down, down, up'. This will enable a smooth transition to the new rising trot and is done in time to the trot rhythm so the balance of horse and rider is not affected. Once you have sat for the extra beat, you can then carry on with the normal rising rhythm of 'up, down'.

Sitting trot

Sitting trot can be very bouncy and definitely requires practice. It helps to be supple in your hip joints and stable in your body to absorb the movement. Sitting trot can be quite tiring if you are not used to it as it requires good posture control from your core abdominal muscles. Your arms will need to stay still in sitting trot and not bounce up and down or this will inadvertently pull on the horse's mouth. Your legs will need to stay relaxed and long down the horse's sides and not creep upwards and grip or you will bounce more and the horse may mistake gripping for a cue to go faster. Some people, who have got used to rising trot and feel comfortable with it, are a bit reluctant to try sitting trot at first, but it is important to master it because, once you have done so, you will find it allows greater control of the horse than rising – and it is a necessary precursor to riding at canter.

A dressage rider performing sitting trot during a test.

To absorb the movement, your pelvis needs to be able to rock gently forward and back in time to the two-time rhythm. Your legs should hang loosely from the hip joints and spine and you must remain in an upright balance. The motion of sitting trot is different from the rising trot as, to achieve the best flow, you need to mirror the motion of down and forwards as the horse's back rises and drops. The best way to feel this is in the walk. Start by over-exaggerating the feeling that your bottom sinks into the saddle, rolls under the seat bones and rises up by the pommel in a down and forwards rolling motion. If you are on the lunge (see Chapter 11) or on a sensible horse, you can also place one hand on a hip joint to make sure you can feel it opening as your legs slightly relax away from the saddle. When back in the trot, aim to start with the horse in a slow trot or jog so you can concentrate on the relaxation of your legs, tallness of your upper body and swinging of your seat.

You can also hold the front of the saddle with one hand to help balance yourself by pulling your weight into the saddle so you are able to relax your legs and control any bouncing that you may experience. Remember, the stiffer your hips are and the more your legs grip on, then the more you will bounce! It is a difficult concept that you do not stay on by strength and gripping but by balance and this will only be achieved through practice and developing core muscle strength. Normally, you will learn the sitting trot by doing a few strides and then going back into rising trot.

INTERESTING FACTS › TYPES OF TROT

There are four types of trot recognised in modern dressage – collected, working, medium, and extended. There are also two movements, called piaffe and passage, seen only at the very high levels of dressage, which are effectively very extreme forms of short trot. Piaffe has high, short steps so the horse looks as though he is trotting on the spot and passage is a very springy shortened form of trot in which the horse looks as though he is bouncing on springs!

A horse and rider performing passage.

Downward transitions

Movements from halt to walk, and from walk to trot as described above are known as upward transitions: downward transitions describe the process of going back 'down through the gears'. For now, we will just look at the transitions from walk to halt, and from trot to walk; the transition down from canter to trot is discussed in Chapter 10.

Walk to halt

Sit tall, and still in your seat and upper body, so that the horse feels a 'passive resistance' to the motion of the walk; close your legs gently and feel the contact a little firmer with both reins. Once the horse has halted, ease the leg and rein contact slightly.

The basic principles for this transition are actually the same for all downward transitions. The gentle closing of the legs encourages the horse's hind legs to step forward under his body, which helps him remain in balance, rather than 'falling' into the transition; the firmer rein contact is the message to go 'down a gear'. Once the horse has made the transition, the aids that requested it are lightened, because he has done what he was asked to do.

Trot to walk

If rising, go into sitting trot and keep your body tall (using the same concept as for walk to halt). Your legs need to feel the horse's sides without pressing as both hands take a non-allowing contact to create a firmer feel on the reins. As the horse returns to walk, soften your hands and allow your elbows to follow the movement of his neck.

Some riding school horses, when ridden by novices, take the downward signal from trot as an excuse to fall into an inactive walk. If the first strides of walk after the downward transition feel laboured, be ready to use your legs to make the walk more active but, once it is, keep them 'quiet' again.

When it goes wrong!

If the horse is not listening to your legs or reins, make the pressure a tiny bit more purposeful without upsetting him. Remember that sudden kicks or pulls are confusing for him. Once you have had a few lessons, you will start to understand how much you can use the aids to get the reaction you desire. However, do remember that every horse is different and some react better or more quickly than others. You will learn to be able to adapt your riding to suit every type of horse. This is called developing 'feel'.

Going straight and turning

Going straight

Both your legs need to be hanging down the sides of the horse near the girth. Their job is to keep the horse's body straight. The reins stay either side of the neck and aim to keep it straight. Imagine the horse is flowing through a tunnel created by your legs and hands. Your weight needs to be central in the saddle while you look straight ahead through the horse's ears.

When it goes wrong!

The horse won't walk in a straight line!
Check that your aids are equal. If the horse tends to always move off to one side, then you will have to use more pressure with the leg on that side to help make him understand he can't fall out past your aid. Make sure you are sitting tall and looking where you need to be going.

Turning, cornering or circling

Sit straight in the saddle with your shoulders and head turned slightly in the direction of travel. The inside leg is placed near the girth and the outside leg slightly behind the girth area. The inside rein, by squeezing, not pulling back, asks for a small amount of bend that corresponds to the size of turn or circle (large circles need less bend than smaller ones) while the outside rein makes sure the horse's shoulder does not bulge outwards. When you are travelling faster, a small check on the outside rein to control the speed on the way into the corner and a closing leg on the way out will help the horse to balance. Think of a car; it has to slightly decelerate on the way into a bend but then can accelerate out and stay under good control.

top left To make a turn, start by turning your head and shoulders a litte in that direction.

top right Place the inside leg near the girth and the outside leg slightly behind it.

lower left Hold the outside rein close to the horse's neck to stop him falling out through his shoulder.

lower right This rider is provoking the horse's shoulder to fall out by asking for too much inside bend.

When it goes wrong!

1. *The horse falls out through his shoulder and his neck is over-bending to the inside!*

   Make sure you have not collapsed your upper body and pulled back on the inside rein, which will cause the bend in the neck. The shoulder falls out because the horse is losing balance or not listening to the outside leg, so increase the feel on his side a little nearer to the girth to help straighten him up. Make sure you have not overturned your body and unbalanced the horse. Also, make sure that you have sufficient contact in your outside rein, as this largely controls the shoulders, but do not overdo this in an attempt to counteract pulling on the inside rein.

2. *The horse is falling in and the turn or circle is getting smaller!*

   Often the horse will have the opposite bend to the direction he is travelling in as well. More inside leg on his ribs behind the girth will make him move outwards with his body. The inside rein can then ask for the correct inside bend while the outside rein maintains the level of contact necessary to make sure his outside shoulder stays on the line of your turn or circle (but not so much contact that the horse's head is pulled to the outside). However, it is important to understand that the inside leg is the most important aid to keep the circle the correct size and shape.

Riding out of a turn and back to a straight line

Make sure that, throughout, you look where you intend to go, as this will lead your shoulders and help you direct the horse.

On the turn, you rein aids and leg aids will be asking for that movement. Once you have nearly finished the turn, both of your legs need to re-position forwards by the girth so you can ride forwards and straight. The reins will also need to be positioned centrally with equal pressure. Plan to be changing your aids from a turn to a straight line before you finish so you control the last few strides and the horse does not overturn and lose balance.

CHAPTER TEN

GOING FASTER – CANTER AND GALLOP

Canter

It is possible for a horse to go into canter from halt, walk or trot, but when you are learning, canter is invariably asked for from trot as the horse will have a bit of power and energy and this makes it easier for you to ask him to go one 'gear' faster. The best place to ask for canter is when you are riding into a corner of the arena. This is because the corner tends to make the horse balance more onto his hindquarters and so he will already have his hind legs more underneath him and more prepared to use the outside hind leg for striking off into canter. If there are the beginnings of correct bend through the corner, this will also make it easier to strike-off on the correct lead.

To prepare for the canter transition, make sure the horse is doing an energetic trot but is not rushing. Go into sitting trot and then ask for the canter on the way into the corner of the school with your inside leg closed by the girth and your outside leg pressing back behind the girth. Sit tall with a soft seat (see Chapter 11 for further explanation) and your shoulders turned a little in the direction of travel. The inside rein needs to ask for a small bend in the horse's neck in the direction he is moving. The outside rein stays close to the outside of the horse's withers to help prevent him from falling outwards and becoming unbalanced.

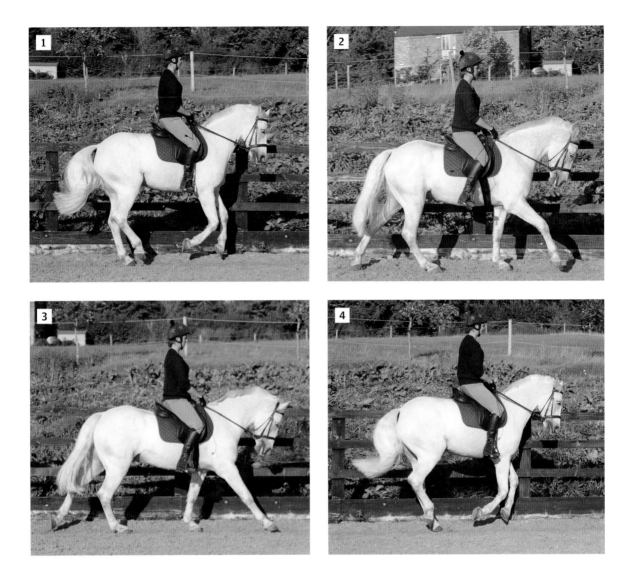

In summary, canter to the right (clockwise): sitting trot is taken before the transition to canter. Remain tall in the saddle with your upper body. Place your inside leg (in this example, your right) on the area by the girth and the outside leg (in this case, your left) about 10cm behind the girth and press gently against the horse's sides. Pressing (advancing) your inside seat bone forward a little will help this aiding. Your outside hand needs to hold the rein close to the horse's neck while the inside hand can bring the rein a little wider on the inside of the horse's neck to help him understand which direction he will be going in – this will hopefully result in him cantering on the correct lead. The opposite aids are applied to ask for left canter.

Sequence of legs at the canter. (Shown here, right lead.)

1 Outside hind.

2 Diagonal pair.

3 Leading foreleg.

4 Moment of suspension.

Once in canter, the feeling is like a gentle rolling action dipping down in front and then dipping down at the back – a little like a see-saw. Canter is normally much smoother than the sitting trot but has a longer stride length and can feel a bit fast when you are not used to it. When you are learning to ride, the horse you ride in your lessons will normally be fairly lazy so that you have to actively make him canter. This will make you confident and also encourage you to use the aids effectively to keep the horse cantering. (As with walk and trot, there is no point in continually 'nagging' the horse in canter, but it is a more complex, more energetic gait than walk and trot and, particularly when going round corners or circles, the horse needs a reasonable amount of activity to maintain balance. Therefore, you should be able and willing to 'support' the horse as necessary by encouraging him to keep active.) Maintaining contact with the saddle can be an issue when you are learning, as canter is ridden seated on the saddle. It helps if you have become reasonably proficient in sitting trot before you start cantering: as with the sitting trot, good balance and core muscles are required to sit securely to the canter. A supple back and seat with good balance and relaxed legs will help you to sit evenly on the horse.

Canter to trot

Rider errors in canter. **left** Rider out of balance in the canter. **right** Rider tipping forwards in canter.

As explained earlier, when describing the walk to halt transition, the idea in a downward transition is to help the horse move into the new gait in a balanced way, and it is a particularly desirable aim when riding

in the faster, asymmetrical gait of canter. Try to think of easing the horse forward into trot, rather than pulling back into it. To make the transition from canter to trot, sit tall in the saddle, using your seat to help modify the forward movement. At the same time, close the legs gently and, with both hands, take the contact a little firmer, with non-allowing hands. The moment the horse returns to trot, make sure your hands soften. Ride the first few strides in sitting trot before reverting to rising.

TOP TIPS > CHECKING THE LEAD

When checking your horse's canter lead, glance down momentarily at the horse's forelegs to see which leg is leading. This is the leg that reaches out furthest past the horse's body and it should be the leg on the inside. When you glance down at the horse's shoulders, you should be able to see the inside shoulder moving more forwards than the outside one. When you are riding on the correct lead it will feel balanced on the turns and corners.

It is also beneficial to watch the other riders in the arena cantering so you are able to identify if their horses are on the correct leg. This visual information can support the development of your own 'feel'.

Galloping

Gallop is very fast and is the gait used extensively for sports such as eventing and hunting, and for racing. During the gallop, the rider does not sit in the saddle but has short enough stirrup leathers so as to be able to raise the seat off the horse's back while keeping the knees bent. The rider needs to fold at their hips so their shoulders are parallel to and above the horse's shoulders. Jockeys do an extreme form of this position; in a more moderate form it is called a light seat as the weight is off the horse's back and this enables him to move faster and with more freedom. Galloping is normally done outside of the arena as the corners make it too tight a turn for the horse at this speed. It is great fun to gallop outside in the country

A rider galloping in a light seat.

but it is a gait for the experienced, as riders must be able to balance their own bodyweight, have enough strength to sustain the position and also be able to control the horse when going flat out. In a similar way to canter, the ideal downward transition (in anything other than an emergency) entails an 'easing down' rather than an abrupt 'pulling up'. You should be confident and competent at cantering in the open before attempting to gallop.

CHAPTER ELEVEN

IMPROVING ON THE LUNGE

One of the best ways to improve your balance and riding ability is to have some private lessons on the lunge. Being on the lunge means that the horse will have a line called a lunge line attached to his bridle (or to a lungeing cavesson, which is worn over a bridle) and your instructor holds the other end. The horse is then asked to go on a circle around the instructor. Because the horse is under the control of the instructor in terms of both direction and speed, you are able to ride him at the same time but do not have to worry about controlling him. It is a great way to feel the movement of the horse, be able to ride with or without stirrups or reins, and to gain more confidence as well as improve your balance and core stability.

During a lunge lesson, the instructor will first warm up the horse by lungeing him on both reins in walk, trot and canter. The horse will have side-reins attached from the girth to the bit. These help to keep him under control and assist him to work with his head fairly low so his back is softer. This makes his movement less bumpy and easier for you to sit on.

To start with, your instructor will make sure you are comfortable with riding on the lunge and you will ride with both reins and stirrups. Once you are confident, the reins are then tied into a knot so you can hold the very end where the buckle joins them with the outside hand. This hand can also hold onto the pommel of the saddle, or a balance strap (a thin

A rider having a lesson on the lunge.

strap secured to the D-rings of the saddle), or a neckstrap, to help you feel secure and balanced without pulling on the horse's mouth. Your inside hand can then hang behind your thigh. A progression of this is to drop the knotted end of the reins onto the horse's neck and this will enable you to do stretches and arm movements. It is a bit like yoga on horseback!

When you are learning more difficult exercises, your instructor will only make you perform them for short periods before gradually building up to doing them for a whole circle or longer. When on the lunge, the instructor will be continually teaching you and will also be interacting with the horse so you will know when the horse is going to be asked to speed up or slow down. This means that you can be prepared and focus on the aim of your lesson – such as staying relaxed in sitting trot.

When you are confident and your instructor thinks you have enough experience, you will also be able to ride without stirrups. Again, the reins are knotted and you can hold the pommel of the saddle to help balance yourself. Riding without stirrups is a good way to help develop balance. You will have to learn to relax your legs and not grip with your knees to become more supple in your seat and able to absorb the motion of the horse.

To help absorb the movement of the horse, your seat will need to become soft and supple. This means that your hip joints (where your legs join into your body) will need to be allowed to slightly open and close in time to the movement of each gait. Your gluteal muscles on your backside also need to be relaxed.

Your legs need to hang without tension but also without any undue wobbling about. Think about the weight of your legs dropping right down through to the feet.

Your body needs to be tall and elegant with your head centrally balanced on top – imagine a tower of little bricks all carefully balanced on top of each other.

Your arms need to be relaxed, with a bend in the elbows. If you find your shoulders creeping upwards with tension, then shrug them up and down to make them looser.

Common exercises on the lunge

Arm exercises

- Circling one arm or both arms forwards or backwards to help loosen your shoulders.

- Stretching both arms upwards or outwards to help improve your body balance and posture.

- Both arms stretched out while rotating your body through the ribcage left and right to help improve upper body flexibility.

- Leaning down to touch your toes to help learn balance, improve confidence and flexibility.

below left Arms over the head.

below right Arms out to the side.

Your instructor will only use a safe horse who is responsive to voice commands and does not mind a rider performing any exercises or being a little unbalanced on his back.

Leg exercises

- Circling your ankles both clockwise and anticlockwise to help loosen them.

- Standing in the stirrups to help leg strength and balance and improve ankle suppleness.

Seat exercise

- Riding without stirrups in walk, trot and canter. An advanced version of this will also include arm exercises at the same time.

Cantering on the lunge with no stirrups and only one hand.

CHAPTER TWELVE

POLE WORK AND BASIC JUMPING

Once you have learnt the basics and are fairly secure in your seat, you can start learning how to jump.

Light seat

As touched on earlier, the light seat is where the rider lifts their weight slightly out of the saddle to help the horse move more freely through his back. Their shoulders are angled a little forwards, with the rider looking straight ahead through the ears of the horse. The rider's weight is balanced by the legs maintaining a slight bend in the hip, knee and ankle joints as it is this bend in the legs that enables the rider to absorb the springiness produced by the horse. The feet need to be firmly secure in the stirrups, with the heels a little lower than the toes and the balls of the feet across the stirrup treads. It is necessary for the stirrup leathers to be shortened by two or three holes to assist the bend in the leg joints and to make it easier for the rider to remain in balance. It also increases the rider's security when using the light seat at fast gaits.

The light seat is used for work over poles, a fast canter or gallop, and for developing rider balance and leg strength. It is also the seat that can be used in between fences when horse and rider are jumping a course of fences.

Pole work

Trotting poles

Trotting poles are introduced to your lessons to help improve your balance and also to start preparing you for jumping.

Normally between three and five poles are used. The space between them should suit the stride length of the horse, a general average being around 1.2–1.4m. The horse moves over them and his footfalls land in between the poles. The purpose of the poles is to encourage him to become more elevated in his gait and improve its regularity. Trotting poles are normally ridden in a light seat. The trot will feel more springy when working over poles.

Canter poles

Canter poles are spaced 2.7 to 3.4 metres apart, again, spaced depending on the stride length of the horse. Canter strides can vary quite a lot, but instructors often use a starting point of about 2.8m. The horse canters over the poles and his footfalls land in between them. The rider can adopt a light seat or a jumping seat. The stirrups need to be shortened two or

Cantering through poles.

three holes from the length the rider would use for riding during flat work, as explained above. The horse will make a larger, more elevated canter stride over each pole so it will feel more like he is jumping over each pole. The canter may feel more bouncy when going over poles.

Progressing to jumping

Jumping seat

The jumping seat is a progression from the light seat and is the adaption made by the rider once the horse has taken off over the fence. The rider folds more from the hips than in the light seat and follows the horse's neck as it stretches out over the fence by allowing their arms to move forwards in the direction of the horse's mouth. The hands can either slide up the neck – this is called a 'crest release' – or follow a straighter line towards the horse's mouth – the 'automatic release'. With the crest release method someone learning to jump can press on the horse's neck to help them balance if they feel insecure, but they should not learn to rely on this as their means of security.

above left Practising the jumping seat at halt.

above right The jumping seat showing the crest release.

left The jumping seat showing the automatic rein release.

The stages of a jump

In the adjacent series of photos, you can clearly see the sequence that horse and rider go through during a jump.

1. **Approach**. The rider and horse are focused on the fence and are approaching in a straight line. The rider has a secure position with head and shoulders upright and lower legs close to the horse to help guide him towards the fence and keep him going actively forwards. The rider's hands are also close and low to keep control of the horse's shoulders and help keep him straight.

2. **Final approach stride before the jump**. The horse lowers his head and prepares to push himself up off the ground.

3. **Take-off**. The horse can now push up into the air as he has brought his hind legs underneath his body. The rider now starts to fold into the jumping seat.

4. **Flight**. The horse has all four feet off the ground. The ideal shape he should make is called a 'bascule', which is the shape of an arch. The rider is positioned centrally just above the horse's back while folding at the hips. This causes the seat to be nearer the back of the saddle and the shoulders to be positioned over the withers and lower part of the horse's neck. The rider's hands and elbows follow the horse's mouth to avoid hardening the rein contact. Ideally, the rider's shoulders should not come forward of their knees when jumping smaller fences.

5. **Landing**. The horse's forefeet stretch out to meet the ground before the hind feet land very close to where the forefeet have been. The rider brings their shoulders upright and the weight down into the heels to re-establish position.

6. **Getaway**. The horse now raises his head and starts to push away from the fence. The rider starts to sit up and adopt a light seat. Horse and rider need to re-balance and re-establish the canter to ride the getaway phase effectively. This is even more important if riding a sequence of fences (a course) or riding through a combination or to a related fence. (A 'combination' is an obstacle consisting of two or three fences – a 'double' or 'treble' – placed only one or two strides apart; 'related' fences are two or more fences within a few canter strides of each other.)

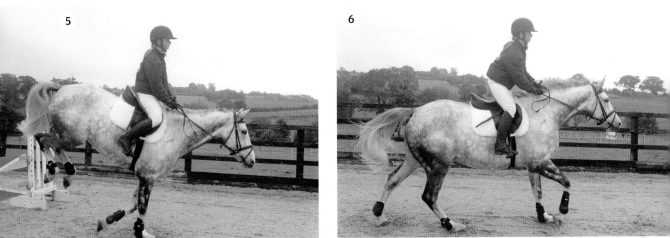

1 The approach. **2** Final stride of the approach. **3** Take-off. **4** Flight. **5** Landing. **6** Getaway.

TOP TIPS > JUMPING

- Being able to go from a light seat to a jumping seat and maintain your balance is a good way to prepare for jumping.

- Looking straight through the ears of the horse will help keep you straight in the saddle.

- Horses require a reasonable amount of energy and activity to jump smoothly. This doesn't mean that they should be rushing, but they should be moving freely forward, so ensure that this is the case before you approach the fence.

- Make sure you focus and ride positively to the fence, and give the horse a squeeze with your legs just before take-off to make it clear that you want him to jump over the obstacle. Some horses will back off if you are hesitant and may end up refusing.

- When going over a fence make sure you keep your hands close to the horse's neck, even when you release and follow his neck. This creates a better balance for you.

- Don't throw your whole bodyweight over the horse's neck when he is taking off as this will unbalance him. Whether you adopt the crest release or automatic release system, you should bear in mind that a rider adapts their posture in the act of jumping solely to remain in balance and harmony with the horse's movement. Over small fences, as jumped by novice riders on school horses, these adaptations need be only quite modest. The aim is to go sufficiently 'with' the horse, but not to fling yourself into exaggerated and insecure positions.

- Make sure you sit up and ride straight after the fence to regain balance and control.

Common jumping problems

1. *Getting 'left behind' the motion of the horse and end up pulling on his mouth.*
   Placing a finger in the neckstrap on the approach will help you stay more in balance and be able to follow the motion of the jump better.

2. *Losing balance over or after the jump.*
   Make sure your stirrup leathers are not too long or too short. You will need to practise moving back and forth between the light seat and the jumping seat to develop the ability to sit up after the jump. Practising standing in the stirrups at halt and progressing to doing this at trot and canter will help get the weight down in your heels and strengthen your legs so you are stronger and more able to regain your balance quickly. However, note that this is a specific exercise for a specific purpose. Straightening your legs during the actual act of jumping is not required and is to be avoided.

3. *Throwing your weight forwards or sideways over the jump.*
   Throwing your weight forwards and getting in front of the movement will unbalance the horse and, as mentioned, is not the same as folding forward in harmony with his movement. Tipping sideways will also unbalance him. Aim to keep looking straight ahead between the horse's ears before, during and after the fence.

4. *Horse runs out before the fence.*
   Make sure both your leg and rein aids are guiding him securely to the centre of the fence. Keep your shoulders back on the approach and don't fold your body until the horse has taken off.

5. *Horse stops in front of the fence.*
   Turn him away and re-present him in a positive manner and on a straight line to the centre. Encourage him to take off by giving him a kick, if necessary backed up by a tap with the stick on the last stride.

CHAPTER THIRTEEN

BECOMING A BETTER RIDER

Fitness and exercises

Having a certain level of fitness before you start will make your initial riding lessons much easier and more enjoyable. Always warm up your muscles before you ride – you wouldn't go for a run without stretching and warming up and the same applies to riding. It will help you stop aching after your lesson.

Warming up

To help your joints and muscles become more supple and ready for exercise, start by gently moving the joints in your arms and legs. Build up from gently rolling your shoulders or rotating your wrists and ankles to adding arm circling and leg swinging.

Arm circling can be done with each arm individually or both arms together. The circling motion is best done from front to back – this will open the shoulder area and loosen the pectoral muscles on the front of your chest. Riding tends to pull your shoulders forwards through holding your arms in front of you and also having a contact on the reins.

For a **single arm stretch** lead with your thumb as you lift the arm to the highest point above your head, then switch to the little finger leading after that point. This loosens the arms, shoulder, neck and upper back. Take care not to arch your back.

For a **double arm stretch** circle both arms backwards as a pair.

Leg swings. A leg swing from side to side will help to loosen and warm up your hip and leg muscles as well as your lower back. Stand facing a wall, making sure you are the length of your forearm away from the wall then, with both of your arms, press onto the wall without tipping forwards. Transfer your weight onto one leg and move the other in a swinging motion, crossing in front of the standing leg, and then out to the side, away from the leg you are standing on. Make sure it is just your leg that moves and not your whole body.

Arm stretches can be a useful part of warming up.

1 Single arm stretch.

2 Double arm stretch.

Swinging the leg sideways to loosen and warm up hip, back and leg muscles.

Swinging the leg forward and back.

Leg swings from front to back will help the hip, pelvis and thigh muscles to loosen up. Stand sideways to a wall and use the hand nearest the wall to rest on for balance. Stand on the leg closest to the wall, and swing the other leg forwards and backwards without losing upper body straightness.

Strengthening and stretching exercises

Riding involves a lot of balance and your legs need to be able to support your bodyweight, especially during rising trot and jumping. Your ankles, knees and hips need to be flexible and capable of opening and closing their angles with good control and suppleness.

Lunges can help to strengthen your calf and thigh muscles. Stand with feet shoulder-width apart. Take a large step forward with one foot, then bend both knees to lower yourself gently. Maintain your upper body balance by keeping your shoulders and hips in line, and make sure that you look forward, with your chin up. Take care not to move too far forward or low – aim to keep your foot in front of your knee and at a 90 degree angle when you are at the lowest point of stretch. Then rise back up.

A **half squat** is a good off-horse exercise to help practise the up and down motion of the rising trot. With your feet shoulder-width apart, look straight ahead and keep your back and pelvis in a straight line, with your tummy button in. Bend your knees and lower yourself down without tipping forwards, and then rise back up again.

Lunges are good for calf and thigh strength. Try to stay upright with the upper body.

Half squats are great practice for rising trot.

Calf stretches and strengthening will benefit you if you have trouble keeping your heels down, have poor ankle mobility or need to improve your leg strength and balance. The easiest way to do these is to stand on a raised object, e.g. stairs, with heels off edge (see photos overleaf). Hold on to something to help stabilise yourself for better balance but do not tip forwards. Keep your back straight, your head up and your knees soft, with your feet shoulder-width apart. Gently lower your weight into

Calf stretches, raising and lowering the heels, can improve leg strength and ankle stability.

your heels to stretch the calf muscle and stand up on your toes to improve strength. This exercise must be done slowly to improve strength and control.

Core exercises. As you progress in your riding, you will become more aware that your core tummy muscles play an important part in controlling your balance. An exercise ball can be used to help improve core, balance and stability on a moving object. Start by sitting on the ball with your back straight, looking ahead so your chin does not drop, and think of drawing your tummy button in towards your spine. At first, aim just to be able to sit there and not wobble from side to side! Progress to lifting one leg off the floor slowly whilst keeping control of your upper body – you may have to start by raising just the heel off the floor.

Here's another core exercise that can be done without an exercise ball. Lie on the floor with both knees bent, then slowly push one heel out along the floor as you straighten that leg. Make sure you do not twist your hips so that your lower abdominal muscles are worked efficiently and evenly.

Try to sit up tall and stay still as you lift one foot off the floor.

This floor exercise will get to work on your core, if done correctly.

A more advanced core workout can be done using a chair (see photos overleaf). Start by lying flat on your back with both legs resting on the seat of a sturdy chair; have your arms straight by your sides. Keep your back flat to the floor by thinking of taking your belly button to the floor behind your spine. With your arms straight and hovering off the floor, gently raise your upper body off the floor, curling forwards towards your chest, without straining your neck. Then lower your head and shoulders back down to the floor without arching your back. An advanced version of this is to perform the same curl-up with your hands behind your head.

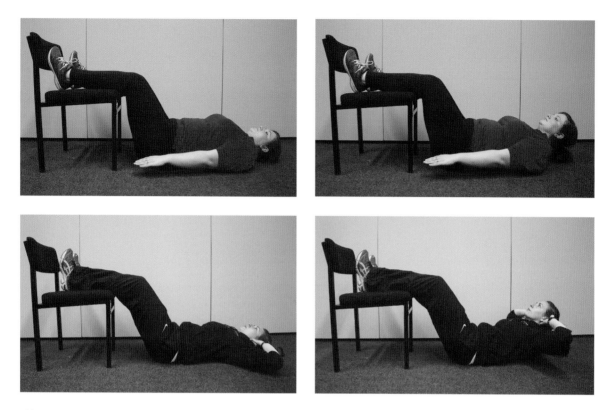

This more advanced core exercise involves curling up with the head and upper body.

This excellent stretch will help release any tightness in the back and hip area.

Stretching. After riding, or when you feel your back is tight, a good stretch to do is one that works on the long back muscles and hip flexors. Lie flat on your back, with your arms out straight to the side and with your knees bent. Make sure you are comfortable, then straighten one leg and roll the bent knee over the straightened leg without letting your shoulders twist or rise off the floor. Repeat on the opposite side.

Coping with fear

Many people are afraid of horses because they are big animals that they know little about and people are very often scared of the unknown.

Fear has the natural positive function of self-protection – fear warns us of danger; it is an alarm signal that we should take seriously.

Horses provide a good illustration of how fear can save life and preserve the species. As creatures of flight, horses react to alarm signals by running away. Without this flight instinct, the horse would not exist.

Even domesticated horses do not have the benefit of human reason and although they are more desensitised to modern-day life than, say, horses that live in the wild, new and uncertain things can scare them.

That said, as a human, with human powers of reasoning, you can come to terms with your fear, first of all by facing up to it, then looking for the reasons behind it. It is perfectly understandable and natural that beginner-riders feel unusually fearful or anxious when faced with such a large animal as a horse. This is normal and is simply fear of the unknown. You can master this fear by spending time with horses, grooming them, leading them and getting as much contact with them as possible before you start your riding lessons.

A good tip is to watch how other people react around horses and concentrate hard on imagining yourself in their place, as if you were doing it.

You may also find relaxation techniques such as deep breathing useful before you make contact with the horse. Communication is key so if you are ever feeling uneasy about something, talk to your instructor. After all, everyone was a beginner at some point and your instructor is there to help you learn, not bully you into doing things you aren't comfortable doing.

The more time you spend with horses and riding them, the more confident you will become. As they say, practice makes perfect!

Learning how to fall

Fear of falling off a horse is perfectly natural and your instructor will do their utmost to avoid you falling, but by learning how to fall, you can be prepared if ever it happens.

There are various steps you can take to assist you to fall as safely as possible. In practice, it has to be said that things may happen too quickly, or you may be concentrating too hard on trying to stay on to give them much considered thought at the time, but if you have a background awareness of these ideas, they may kick in subconsciously to your benefit.

Relax – however hard it may seem, the more tense you are, the more likely you are to land awkwardly and injure yourself. Relaxing will enable your body to absorb the fall.

Tuck and roll – when you are falling try to remember to tuck your head in and roll over your shoulder out of the way of the horse. It is particularly worthwhile trying to get this concept into your subconscious, because it may save you from sticking an arm out and damaging your wrist or collarbone.

Reins – people instinctively try to keep hold of the reins when falling and, in certain situations, this is understandable. However, it is potentially very dangerous, especially if the horse is excitable or frightened, or if you are in close company with other horses.

Check for injury – once you've landed, don't just jump straight up and go running after your horse. Check that you aren't badly injured and get help if you feel pain anywhere.

There are now courses available on teaching riders how to fall – alternatively, it may be possible to obtain valuable advice from a martial arts teacher.

CHAPTER FOURTEEN

RIDING OUT

Enjoying the countryside from the back of a horse is one of the great things about riding. Hopefully, by the time you go on your first hack (as riding out is called), you will have all the basics in place and will be able to control your horse safely.

Riding out on hacks is very different from riding in an arena. The horses are more likely to find things to be excited or afraid about, such as plastic bags and big, noisy vehicles, so it's important that you know how to control the horse if such a situation arises. Therefore you should not go out hacking unless you are ready and the horse you start hacking on should be experienced and quiet out on the roads. A good riding centre will assess these issues and novice hacks should always be accompanied by an appropriate number of experienced staff.

Although there is plenty for you to look at out on hacks, it's important that you stay aware at all times. Think ahead and be on the lookout for potentially frightening or dangerous situations.

You'll come across all different types of terrain and obstacles out hacking, such as big open fields, hills and forests. Remember that you are a lot taller on a horse so be aware of low-lying branches or narrow spaces when riding through woods.

When riding uphill, take a light seat and shift your weight forwards slightly to allow your horse to use his back end to push him up the hill.

A family enjoying a hack in open countryside.

Keep your lower legs underneath you to support you and keep them closely against your horse's sides. It's quite common for horses to want to trot up hills because going up is hard work for them, but try to stay with the movement so you don't lose your balance and jab your horse in the mouth with the reins. When going downhill, always stick to walk and sit back slightly to take the weight off your horse's shoulders. However, when you do this be careful that you don't increase the rein contact because the horse will need some freedom of his neck to assist his balance.

Sometimes, being in open spaces can be very exciting for horses, especially if they are with a group of others. Windy weather can also make horses more jumpy because the leaves on the trees will rustle and move around, and litter may be blown about, so take care when riding in strong winds. Try to stay calm and quiet and don't panic if they suddenly take off. Have a firm hold of the reins, but don't simply pull back as this won't have much of an effect. Instead, give and take the reins (this means change the amount of contact on one rein at a time, so one hand holds the contact firm while the other slightly reduces then increases it, then the hands swap roles). If space allows, make a circle to try to regain control. Use your voice to try to calm your horse if he has been spooked.

Be aware of the ground conditions when you're out hacking. If it's been raining, the ground may be slippery or tacky, which can injure the horse if he slips or gets stuck in the deep going. Riding in icy or snowy

above Riding in open spaces can be exciting and fun for both horse and rider.

left Two riders in hi-vis clothing enjoying a canter in an open field.

conditions is potentially very dangerous, as horses can easily slip on icy surfaces, especially if wearing shoes. You should never knowingly venture out in such conditions (and riding centres should be aware of this), but they can sometimes come on unexpectedly and, if you are caught in them, you should proceed with great caution. Similarly, if the ground is rough and uneven, take it steady to give your horse a chance of picking his way through safely. Riding along grass verges can be dangerous as there is often hidden rubbish that could harm your horse, or open drains and uneven ground that are hidden under the grass.

Riding out is even more enjoyable when accompanied by a friend. (Very novice riders should be accompanied by stable staff).

Summer is a great time of year for riding out on hacks, but hard, baked ground is dangerous if ridden over at speed as it can jar the horse's legs and joints.

It's always advisable to ride with other people when hacking out in case something untoward happens. Always carry a mobile phone in an arm or leg band (have an ICE – in case of emergency – number programmed into it) and let someone at the yard know where you are going and how long you are likely to be.

When practical, choose the middle of the day to go hacking. It's usually quieter on the roads in the middle of the day as opposed to the morning or evening rush hours. It also means that you should have plenty of daylight.

Be respectful if you ride over other people's land, even if it is a bridle-path or right of way. Make sure you close all gates behind you (see page 150) and walk slowly and quietly through fields of livestock. Be aware of dog walkers and cyclists who might share the same routes – they have as much right to be there as you and may be intimidated by horses, so slow down and give them plenty of room to pass you.

If it is a dreary or foggy day, it's essential that you wear hi-vis gear such as a fluorescent tabard or rug on your horse so that you are easily seen – and this is advisable on other occasions too. It gives other road users plenty of time to see you on the road (see also next section) and you will be much easier to find if you fall off and people need to come looking for you. BHS-approved centres nowadays ensure that this equipment is used.

Road safety

When you ride on the road, remember that you are sharing it with other road users such as cars, bikes and walkers. You have a responsibility to these other road users so it's vital that you can control your horse and stay safe.

Quiet, winding country lanes are often the most dangerous because cars come whizzing around the corners without enough time to see you and slow down. Therefore, it's vital that you wear reflective, hi-vis gear to give them every opportunity to spot you before it's too late. It's amazing how even the lightest coloured horse can easily blend into the shadows on a dreary day.

Wearing hi-vis clothing will ensure you are seen by other road users.

Unfortunately, many drivers don't appreciate that horses can become scared of cars and it's our responsibility as horse riders to be thankful when they do slow down and give us plenty of space. If you are polite to them, they are more likely to be courteous to other riders.

There are a few basic rules when riding on the road – always ride on the left-hand side of the road and, on narrow or busy roads, ride in single file, unless you have a young or frightened horse who needs an older, more experienced horse next to him.

If a horse or rider is inexperienced on the road, it is good practice to ride side-by-side, with a more experienced companion to the outside. It's also fine to do so on quiet roads, but be aware of other road users and don't hold them up by 'hogging' the road for no good reason.

Horses don't have indicators, so it's up to you to tell other road users where you are intending to go. If you need to turn left, hold your left arm straight out as you approach the junction and similarly, if you need to turn right, hold out your right hand. Make sure you give your signals in plenty of time and that they are clear. When giving hand signals, take both reins in the hand that is not signalling and make sure that you don't wave your whip around near the horse's head and risk spooking him.

To thank drivers, simply hold up your hand and smile with a nod. If you don't feel it is safe to take your hand off the reins, a smile and a nod will suffice.

The *Highway Code* has a section on riding on the road and the BHS runs a Riding and Road Safety Test, and training for and taking this can provide valuable information and experience relevant to safe practice on the highway. Many approved centres offer these tests, and further information can be obtained from such centres, or directly from the BHS.

opposite below Thanking other road users for passing wide and slow.

Making a hand signal to
turn left.

TOP TIPS › OPENING A GATE

It is really useful to be able to open and shut a gate when you are mounted on a horse. It means you don't have to get off when on a hack and there may not be a suitable place for you to remount from.

To open the gate, first line the horse up parallel to the gate with his head at the end that opens.

Take both your reins into the outside hand and, with the hand nearest the gate, take hold of the latch and lift it to release the gate.

Take hold of the gate and push it open as you ask the horse to walk slowly forwards. Make sure the gate does not accidentally close on the horse and make sure you open it enough for him to fit through without catching your legs on the post or gate.

Once the horse's shoulders are through the gap, begin to slow his front end with the reins and ask him to step his hindquarters around the gate by using your outside leg. Ideally the horse's hindquarters move through 180 degrees and you are able to keep control of the gate with the same hand.

However, if there is not enough room for the horse to move round or you lose your hold on the gate, then, when the gate is open wide enough, ride him forwards through the gap, then reposition him next to the gate and reach out, take the gate and place the latch back securely.

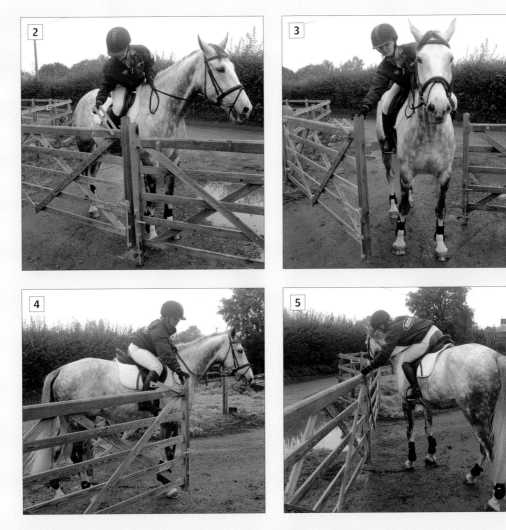

How to ride through a gate.

1 To open a gate, first line the horse up with the gate.

2 Take both reins in the hand away from the gate and take hold of the gate latch with the other hand.

3 Lift the latch and ask the horse to move forwards through the gate.

4 Keep hold of the gate and ask your horse to move around it.

5 Push the gate closed, keeping hold of it at all times, and place the latch back on the gate to secure it.

CHAPTER **FIFTEEN**

WHAT'S NEXT?

Once you are at a competent level and your instructors feel you have grasped the basics, there's a lot more you can do outside of lessons.

Riding holidays are a great way to spend time with friends and visit new places. Whether it's here in the UK, or further afield abroad, riding holidays offer you the best of both worlds – a vacation from everyday life, and horse-riding all in one. You'll find plenty of riding holiday options on the internet but make sure you go through a reputable travel agent so that you are suitably insured. Word of mouth is a great way of finding somewhere that is well-run with healthy, happy horses who will look after you.

Another option is trekking, where you turn up at a centre and go riding around the vicinity to take in the local wonders on horseback. The length of time you go out for can vary but you will be sure to see some amazing landscapes off the beaten track.

Riding centres will have suitable horses for most levels of rider, but be honest about your ability. The last thing you want to do is be partnered with a horse who is too much for you and end up having a bad experience.

If you are interested in learning more about caring for horses as well as riding, ask about opportunities to help out at your local riding school or yard. You will need to have adequate insurance, but it is a great way for you to learn all about the day-to-day care of horses.

Another good way of learning and gaining experience is to take BHS exams. These come in various forms: the 'grade' system is really aimed at people who might want to work professionally with horses, but there is also a series of exams administered by the Riding Clubs arm, and a series of progressive riding tests is available through BHS-approved centres. The common factor of this system is that you will be taught by qualified BHS trainers and be examined, after which you will receive a certificate if you pass, and can then progress to the next level if you wish to do so. The ABRS also has a system of horse care and riding tests.

Your riding school may also hold frequent competitions in dressage and showjumping, or even cross-country. Some centres will loan you a horse to compete on to give you the experience of competition on a safe, well-schooled horse. There may also be options for a more regular share or loan of a horse at your riding school, which will give you further experience of looking after a horse. There are plenty of options based on such arrangements, such as helping to care for a horse or pony for a few days a week while you learn the ropes.

Buying a horse or pony of your own should not, however, be done lightly. They are a huge responsibility and only experienced people should consider taking one on. It can take years to accrue enough knowledge to be suitably qualified to care for a horse, and loaning or sharing is a great way of learning these skills while being supported by more experienced people around you. If you do consider buying a first horse or pony, it is a good idea to keep him at a knowledgeable livery yard, where plenty of support should be available.

Take part is as many activities as you can. Group lessons, private lessons, clinics, hacks, riding different horses and competitions will all add to your experience and skills base. Remember, riders never stop learning.

USEFUL ADDRESSES

British Horse Society
Abbey Park
Stareton
Kenilworth
Warwickshire
CV8 2XZ

www.bhs.org.uk

Association of British Riding Schools
Unit 8, Bramble Hill Farm
Five Oaks Road
Slinfold
Horsham
West Sussex
RH13 0RL

www.abrs-info.org

The Pony Club
Stoneleigh Park
Kenilworth
Warwickshire
CV8 2RW

www.pcuk.org

British Dressage
Meriden Business Park
Copse Drive
Meriden
West Midlands
CV5 9RG

www.britishdressage.co.uk

British Eventing
Abbey Park
Stareton
Kenilworth
Warwickshire
CV8 2XZ

www.britisheventing.com

British Showjumping
Meriden Business Park
Copse Drive
Meriden
West Midlands
CV5 9RG

www.britishshowjumping.co.uk

INDEX